THE PENGUIN CLASSICS

EDITED BY E. V. RIEU

L92

D0756665

SIR GAWAIN AND THE GREEN KNIGHT

TRANSLATED
WITH AN INTRODUCTION BY
BRIAN STONE

PENGUIN BOOKS

Penguin Books Ltd, Harmondsworth, Middlesex
U.S.A.: Penguin Books Inc., 3300 Clipper Mill Road, Baltimore 11, Md
AUSTRALIA: Penguin Books Pty Ltd, 762 Whitehorse Road,
Mitcham, Victoria

—

This translation first published 1959

—

Made and printed in Great Britain
by The Whitefriars Press Ltd
London and Tonbridge

CONTENTS

INTRODUCTION

SOME disapprove of English literature written after about 1350 being translated at all. They believe that an intelligent person who is curious enough to pick up the book in the first place should be satisfied with a scholarly edition of the original, attractively printed and accompanied by a glossary. But even if this were true of some works, there are others which will never be read outside the universities unless they are translated. A glance at the last appendix in this volume will show the reader at once how much of a student he would have to become in order to enjoy *Sir Gawain and the Green Knight* in the original. It can scarcely be thought surprising that such a work, written in a language which seems as remote from Chaucer's as Chaucer's is from ours, is not well known to the general public. Yet prose fairy-tale versions, duly bowdlerized, do exist in collections of Arthurian romances made for children, so that more than one person to whom I have mentioned my work has raked memory to unearth the terrifying appearance of the Green Knight, rolling his red eyes. There are also full translations, but they are hard to come by, and none that I have read is both in modern English and in the original metre: this is what I seek to supply. I know it is presumptuous to attempt in one language what has already been perfected in another, but this is a charge which every translator must face. 'The question is not,' wrote Newman, 'What translator is perfect? but, Who is least imperfect?' In my note on this translation I adumbrate my hopes and confess my failures, while showing to the curious and exposing to the quizzical the method of one who, whatever his shortcomings may be, is concerned to render the meaning and spirit of the poem as closely as his terms of reference permit.

Sir Gawain and the Green Knight is the masterpiece of medieval alliterative poetry, and the finest poem of the age outside Chaucer's works. It is so different from anything in Chaucer that comparison is impossible; certainly neither Chaucer nor any succeeding English poet wrote a narrative poem of such extraordinary richness. Beside the refined, almost Greek, simplicity of Chaucer's language, the ornamented verse of the contemporary north-western poet rears like a Hindu temple, exotic and densely fashioned. Its outlandish quality derives partly from its language, and partly from its expression of an early medieval northern culture which was to be largely submerged in a rival culture, the one based on the London-Oxford-Cambridge triangle and destined to become ours. But exotic though it may be, there is nothing sprawling or inorganic about the poem, although the genre of the Romance has produced some of the least shapely works in literature. At a perfect moment in English literary development, when the spirit of the Middle Ages is fully alive but has not long to last, the poet has again brought to life the heroic atmosphere of saga, with its grim deeds and threatening landscapes; has absorbed into traditional English poetic form the best of the finesse and spirit of French romance; and thrown over all his elements, with their shadowy pagan base material, the shimmering grace of his Christian consciousness. The result is a Romance both magical and human, powerful in dramatic incident, and full of descriptive and philosophic beauty; in which wit, irony, and occasional pathos provide subtle variety.

Some scholars have not felt able to credit a fourteenth-century north-western English poet with the sense of form needed to create *Sir Gawain*. Familiar with the comparative barbarity of inferior romances, into which marvels and adventures of all sorts were haphazardly fitted without regard to the need for a strong narrative line, they have inferred the existence of a French original. An argument in favour of this thesis seemed to be provided by the assurance of the poet in his treatment of the typically French romance elements, those concerned with the manners of the court and the love passages between Sir Gawain and the Lady. Unfortunately, no French original exists, so that the theory concerning it is a slight to the poet, which no generous acknowledgement of his improvement on the supposed source can mitigate.

It is the successful way in which the poet has subordinated the French courtliness to its place in an English setting that convinces me of the originality of the work: no grafting on of elements is apparent, for the attitude of the guiding mind remains consistent, whether the hero is being 'half-slain by the sleet' or 'invited to the very verge' by the Lady. We may allow the direct French inspiration of the love scenes, but when we find in the poem full descriptions of English period clothing, armour, and architecture (the poet's confident sophistication has led more than one scholar to suggest that he may have been a member of John of Gaunt's entourage), an almost Norse sense of desolate nature, and a pervasive loftiness of moral tone which is not characteristically French, we must surely admit that the poet was capable of conceiving the whole work. The grand design, no less than the beauty of the parts, proclaims the author a poet of genius.

The source of the poem's main plot, that concerning the Beheading Game, appears to have been the Irish epic of Fled Bricrend, in one episode of which Cuchulain agrees to play the Beheading Game with Uath mac Imomain (Terror, son of Great Fear): Cuchulain strikes off Uath's head, and when he comes back next day to offer his own head, Uath strikes three blows without hurting him and declares him a champion. The second main component theme, that of the Temptation by the Lady, seems to have no precise original, but tests of the chastity of Arthur's knights, and even of Gawain, are so common that there would be little profit in looking for an exact analogue in which it is the host's wife who is the instrument of temptation. It is worth noting that our poet shows a good deal more delicacy in dealing with the subject than the writers of the approximate analogues. The Exchange of Winnings, the third component theme, by which the poet so well combines the stories of the two tests, is not found anywhere in precise form; but again, exchange of gifts is a sufficiently commonplace gambit in the courtesy game.

On both sides of the shadowy frontier which fails to divide pagan myth from medieval Christianity, the land has, through the centuries, been largely claimed by the Church; modern anthropology has steadily reduced the extent of the land claimed, and some critics have been at pains to interpret the Romances, and among them *Sir Gawain*, in terms of pagan ritual, in spite of the often declared Christian purpose of the writers. It is easy to say that both sides are right, but they are, if one accepts Mr Hugh Ross Williamson's argument in *The Arrow and the Sword*: that it is no disservice to the Church to draw attention to the primitive non-Christian influences on Christianity. Such exposures are in complete harmony with the idea of progressive revelation. To put it quite straightforwardly, the Crucifixion and Resurrection gain in force and meaning from the persistence, in pre-Christian myth, of the idea of the slain and resurrected god; the authenticity of *Sir Gawain* as a medieval Christian poem is not in doubt merely because the Green Man is vital to certain fertility cults, or because our hero, even as represented in the poem, still retains some of the attributes of a sun-god or a re-born fertility deity. It is the result of the metamorphosis, the transfiguration of the elements, that counts in both cases. For this reason, I have expressed my interest in the pagan material underlying the poem in the notes and appendices, and not here. A full 'fertility ritual' interpretation, with only some aspects of which I agree, is to be found in Mr John Speirs's *Medieval English Poetry*. When, as I believe, the poet is hardly aware of the sources of some of his material, any attempt to find a consistent parallel to a lost ritual, or to a ritual preserved only in remote places by an inexact racial memory, is bound to break down at some point. The ritual plan of *Sir Gawain* (roughly speaking, of the sacrificed fertility god's being resurrected and re-fertilizing the waste land after winter) is like a Roman road on a modern map: for a few miles it stands out, still a main road, but then it becomes a lane or a grass track, and may vanish altogether for a great distance before re-appearing as the main road.

We must turn to *Sir Gawain*, then, as to a poem in which a Christian knight's courage, good faith, courtesy, and chastity, during two main and various subsidiary ordeals, are celebrated, to the glory of the House of Arthur and the Britain which thought of Arthur as its first great hero. It is above all a Christian poem, on the one hand extolling the temporal and spiritual joys of the season and the society which expressed them, and on the other representing marvellous adventures in the world of dark terror that all knew to exist beyond their hospitable castle walls. The poet's didactic purpose, however, makes itself evident only at the end of the poem, because the reader has been fully engaged in sympathy with the hero in his adventures and diverted by the descriptions of colourful courts, teeming hunts, and desolate landscapes. The close of the poem, with its anti-climax at the Green Chapel and apparently perfunctory explanation of the magical business, followed by Gawain's short lament for his lost virtue, has brought hard words from some modern critics. Yet it is here that the poet explains the end of his Romance. In the atmosphere of lowered tension brought about by the certainty of Gawain's safety, when the cultivated people for whom the poem was obviously written had stilled their heart-beats and could free their minds to receive the lesson this work of art was to bring them, we are offered a decorous conclusion: the hero, faced by a superhuman task, succeeded as nearly as a human being may. His peers, congratulating him on having brought them honour, adopt the green baldric as their badge; but he himself is left lamenting, because the degree by which he failed to reach perfection must be felt by him to the end of his days as 'a tarnishing sin'. The anti-climax, as after the killing of Thomas in *Murder in the Cathedral*, is deliberate. But Eliot rises to rhapsody again before he sends us from the theatre, and here, we may say to our poet as the Green Knight said to Sir Gawain, 'You flagged somewhat, sir'. Certainly the modern reader could bear something like a ceremonial apotheosis of Sir Gawain when he is re-united with the court at Camelot; possibly a description of the court celebrations, parallel to the ecstatic account of them, which has Guinevere at its centre, in the first part of the poem. It would have fitted the poet's pattern, which is circular, the last alliterative line echoing the first.

This pattern of the poem shows a most harmonious balance, sometimes between contrasts and sometimes between correspondences. Thus all is warm and Christian where the courtly writ runs, as at Camelot, but the north, where Gawain goes for his ordeal, is cold and mysterious. Yet the northern castle, if it is effectively to play its role in the temptation of Gawain, must be a simulacrum of Arthur's. Hence, since it is the scene of the struggle for Gawain's chastity and good faith, the impression it leaves on the reader's mind is more powerful than that left by Camelot, whose splendours may be taken for granted because they are recounted in many a romance. The abode of Sir Bertilak, accordingly, when Gawain first saw it, 'shimmered and shone through the shining oaks', although a moment before, in the same wood, the knight was aware of the miserable birds that 'piteously piped away, pinched with cold'. And when Sir Gawain left the castle on his quest to the Green Chapel, he was barely off the end of the drawbridge before he 'climbed by cliffs where the cold clung'.

The long third section, devoted to the three hunts and Sir Gawain's temptation by the Lady, shows the most remarkable patterning. The details of the various hunts are exactly according to hunting usage as laid down in the oldest hunting treatise in English (*The Master of Game*, which was written by Edward, Duke of York, early in the fifteenth century), yet the poet has so selected from and worked on his material that each hunt is an allegory of a parallel stage of the

Lady's attempt to seduce Sir Gawain. Thus the account of the first hunt opens with the terror-stricken deer darting down to the dales at the din of hound and horn; and before the hunt is concluded, we are taken to Gawain's chamber and shown the knight in trepidation at the Lady's unexpected and sudden assault. The second hunt, in which the quarry is 'a baneful boar, of unbelievable size', provides the fiercest encounter for Sir Bertilak and his men, and it is Sir Gawain's second visit from the Lady that drives him to almost desperate verbal shifts in order to maintain his chastity without showing discourtesy. This time his very chivalry is called in question. And in the third hunt, it is the wily and devil-companioning fox that is the victim. The pursuit is all twists and turns, just like the last bedside conversation between the Lady and Sir Gawain. At one point, the fox and the knight alike seem to have escaped, but the fox, having eluded the main hue and cry, lights unluckily on a dog-base, and Sir Gawain, having finally turned the Lady's love-longing into apparent grief for unrequited love, falls into the sin of accepting from her a talisman. Sir Bertilak's disgust with the fox's skin parallels the savour of Sir Gawain's little deception in concealing the gift of the girdle.

Convincing though Sir Gawain is as a character, whether full of foreboding on his first sight of the Green Chapel, or self-deprecating when he relieves King Arthur of the challenge of the Green Knight, it is the Green Knight who is the greater creation. His two selves correspond wonderfully, but such is the poet's skill that the reader not in possession of the final clue can no more than guess at the significance of the correspondences. Physical resemblances are obvious, but the full-blooded, lofty courtesy of the knightly self and the fierce uncouthness of the supernatural being come only afterwards to be seen as 'blossoms upon one tree'. The high moment when the Green Knight waves his beard before Arthur's court, in a stillness so intense that all hear him clear his throat, matches in splendour the moment when the Host and the boar plunge into the stream together, the boar dead, the man exulting. The diabolical mocking of the Green Knight balances the unmalicious quipping of the Lord of the northern castle. Even in his most domestic moments Sir Bertilak is sounding the ground bass to the Green Knight theme. Uproarious, self-delighting, and unreflecting, the double figure makes an impact like a force of Nature. His humour, his love of the hunt and of the chivalric life, make added sense when the mask at last falls, and the Green Knight, the terrible enchanter, compliments the Christian on his virtue. Now, almost wistfully, in his mind's eye he sees the hero thronging in company 'with paragons of princes', and sadly accepts Gawain's refusal to return to his castle. But we are reminded of the omnipresence of evil by the uncanny dismissal of the Green Knight from the story to an undefined but wide realm of activity – 'wherever he would elsewhere'.

It is this ability of the Faerie to span the chasm between Heaven and Hell that makes some of the Romance enchanters more interesting than regular devils with mottoes like 'Evil, be thou my good'. These may behave with a daemonic singleness of purpose which bludgeons the reader into terror, but the enchanters, being shape-shifters and servants to both Ormuzd and Ahriman, keep their mystery. The Lady, as I argue in a note, is a stock enchantress of the school of Morgan the Fay, though she transcends her models in the hands of our poet; but she is so confoundingly attractive that at one moment – and it is the only moment in the whole poem – the poet has almost to give the show away by warning us that she has 'some other motive besides' love in wishing to seduce Sir Gawain. The reader is much with her, therefore, when she runs to his bedside 'in a ravishing robe that reached to the ground'; and he believes in her sincerity when, bidding Sir Gawain farewell, she commends him to Christ 'with cries of chill sadness'. Yet Gawain would certainly have lost his head had she prevailed. Perhaps there existed in those days an unacknowledged apprehension that evil was intimately related to good, rather than a hostile entity; a catalytic agent which, even when the reaction it wished to foster did not take place, could still appreciate and admire what happened instead: so that among those blowing trumpets for Sir Gawain when he triumphs are to be found the grisly headsman of Hell and the sister of Sin herself.

A NOTE ON THE TRANSLATION

TRANSLATORS into modern English of our old poetry have before them two alternatives. One is that represented by Ezra Pound's rendering of the Anglo-Saxon *The Seafarer,* in which a new idiom, strongly suggesting the terrible bare force of the original, and true to it in metre and substance, is hammered out. The other is that represented, broadly speaking, by the Penguin Classics publications, in which the style is that of a modern man speaking to men without artifice. Pound's poetic archaism somehow manages to capture the inflected concentration of old English, and therefore rings hard and true. But archaism will not do for *Sir Gawain* because the syntax of the original, as distinct from the vocabulary, is already almost modern: better to print the original in modernized spelling, with accompanying glossary, than to offer a few arty archaisms and call the result translation. Nor will plain modern English suffice; because *Sir Gawain* is a highly-wrought poem of great elegance and rich colour, so rich that at times one feels the need to have every episode and scene embroidered in tapestry: the poet himself created a special poetic diction, in which conscious archaism played some part. Plain English (in the Wordsworthian sense) would kill both the poem's harsh force and its sumptuous artistry.

I have therefore tried to hit off a style somewhat more embellished than that of good modern prose, but to avoid words rarer or older than those commonly found in Shakespeare and the Bible. Yet I must admit that what emerged in my first draft as something near archaism has occasionally been allowed to stand, when it seemed more effective than any more modern rendering I could devise. In the absence of a generally accepted modern poetic diction, I have felt my way among the words of our language, with their rapidly shifting values, using what I believe to be the feeling and force of *Sir Gawain* as a touchstone.

Accordingly, the reader of the original poem will miss in my version the conglomerations of harsh consonants which give *Sir Gawain* its epic northern vigour. There is something altogether softer about my translation; but when taxed with this, I shall reply that the loss of force is the result of no intention of mine, but rather of a change in the nature of the English language during the last six hundred years. I could go further, and point out that it was not this poet's language, but Chaucer's, which eventually developed into ours.

This admission that it is impossible to do full justice to *Sir Gawain* in translation safely out of the way, it is worth considering what was done. The great problem was the metre. The orthodox English alliterative line, which is the staple line of our poem, has three accented alliterative words, two before the caesura and one after. The poet often exceeds this minimum of alliterating words, but only about a hundred times does he fall short of it. But he avails himself of some useful variants. Thus, a vowel alliterates with any other vowel, or with 'h' (that is staple Old English practice); related consonants, such as 'f' and 'v' may alliterate; dominant letters in groups of consonants may alliterate with their like or with single letters ('p' and 'sp'). Often he uses the unalliterated last word of one line to set the alliterating letter for the next. Enjambement is rare, and most of the lines have feminine endings. Finally, he allows himself such freedom in the distribution and number of the unaccented syllables that it is not possible to state a rule, though the reader will feel that a kind of galloping rhythm (too flexible to be called anapaestic, too marked to be ignored) underlies the whole poem. However, this beat of the alliterative line is most felicitously broken at the end of each stanza, which the poet rounds off with a 'bob' (one iambic foot in a line by itself) and a 'wheel' (a quatrain of three-footed lines), rhyming *ababa* and with internal alliteration in each line of the quatrain.

Such metrical complexity naturally prevented me from writing a verse crib, even if such a thing were possible when dealing with the simplest Romance metre. Some of the lines, which happened to contain words that have kept their meaning, translated themselves, and there were some others which looked as if they needed little modification. But if they had to be changed at all, I was at once faced with the necessity of finding three words of the right meaning and decorum, all beginning with the same letter and occurring in positions where the stress could harmoniously fall. Such a line occurs in stanza IV of Part I, where it is recorded of Arthur's nobles that, after distributing largesse, they gave each other presents, and

> De-bated busyly aboute tho giftes.

Nothing could be easier for the modern reader to understand, nothing (I found) harder to translate. 'Gifts' had to go at once because it had occurred in the previous line; the modern mind is more sensitive than the medieval to casual repetition. Rightly or wrongly, I found that the modern meaning of 'debated' imparted too reflective a sense to the line; and so the whole original line had to be rejected, though it is clearly not bad. I began with

> Commented keenly on these contributions.

But 'contributions' are responses to a pulpit plea for funds, and as I had no other 'c' word, I had to think again.

> Earnestly argued about these offerings

came next. But the tetchiness of 'argued' was foreign to the good feeling of Arthur's lords and ladies. So ('Cheerfully chaffed each other about these charities' having given me a feeling of surfeit) I tried

> Cheerfully chatted about these charities.

This seemed fairly reasonable, although I was not happy about 'chatted'. Then when I pondered 'charities' again, I realized that the word did not describe the nature of the donations. I went back to my previous version in something like despair, but when one of my readers queried it, I had to consider the line afresh, because I had never really approved of it myself. It is worth noting that none of these versions is better than the original line written in modern English, and one or two are clearly worse. Rejecting all the dominant letters I had used so far, I started all over again, and decided that the problem could be solved only by altering the syntax.

Bustling and bantering about these offerings

thus became my final version. There I have the good cheer and the chaffing, and the high sense of movement implied but not stated in the original; but it is still not perfect because, unless it is read with care, the 'about' follows 'bustling' as well as 'bantering', although it belongs to 'bantering' alone. Such striving often led to such partial satisfaction.

This testimony to the difficulty of translating a single alliterative line has been made so long because the problem is rare. But the task of finding a precise English equivalent for any foreign word, even a medieval English one, is familiar to all language students, and I give one example only, in case there is a general reader to whom such matters are new. When Sir Gawain is about to set out on his quest for the Green Chapel, the people who see him off lament that such a promising knight must go to be beheaded by 'an aluish mon'. 'Aluish' is of course our word 'elvish', which is the sole word given by both the glossaries I used. But Puck is elvish, fairies are elfin. 'Supernatural' things are categorized and unromantic, 'spectral' and 'ghostly' describe Gothick apparitions, and 'uncanny' has become debased; while 'fiendish' is too precise. What word, meaning the same as 'aluish', remains to describe this powerful physical presence, so obviously more than human? I plumped for 'unearthly', and my pleasure at finding the right word was modified by a conviction that, although the word was right, the line did not now flow as it ought.

The 'bob' and 'wheel', thick with rhyme and alliteration, usually forced me to demolish the original plan, but in the effort to rebuild faithfully I have generally used all the old bricks; on the whole, these intricate stanza-endings have given me the most pleasure and pain.

One refinement of the poet's has had to go by default: there is no way of indicating in modern English the difference between the formal 'ye' and informal 'thou' of the original, a matter about which the poet was precise. Dr Day writes: 'The singular was used in prayer. Otherwise "ye" is used to superiors, who in turn say "thou", as in the talk between Arthur and Gawain, Gawain and the porter, and Gawain and the servant. But when Gawain says that at all risks he must keep his promise, the servant shows his contempt by using the singular. Between equals the plural is used for politeness, on ceremonial occasions, but in his uncouthness the Green Knight "thou's" Arthur, and the king answers him in the same way. For host and guest the plural is the correct form.... When the Green Knight has disclosed himself to be Gawain's host, he on the whole continues to use the singular, dropping into the more ceremonious plural when he utters his mild rebuke. Gawain, overwhelmed by his discovery of the plot, uses the singular, almost the only mistake he makes in the whole poem. To the Lady of the castle he speaks in the plural (as does Arthur to Guinevere). She is less consistent. In the first interview she twice interpolates a tentative "thou" ... in the second she uses "thou" without any pretext, and in the third she boldly begins with it. But only once ... is she able to inveigle him into saying "thou" to her.'

The poet is prodigal in change of tense, and it is rarely possible to affirm that he moves from past historic to present in order to gain dramatic immediacy. I have therefore felt free to use the past tense nearly the whole time.

The reasons for my use of other devices, such as freely introducing conventional epithets like 'brave' and 'courteous', and varying common subjects like 'man' and 'knight', will appear to the reader, but one radical departure of mine from accepted usage perhaps requires an explanation. This is my rendering in English of the accepted French cognomens of the characters, by which process Sir Dodinal le Savage becomes Sir Dodinal the Fierce, and Mador de la Port Mador of the Gate. My first reason was this: the poem, like the original, is written to be declaimed, and as every memory I have of a poetry reader suddenly having to cope with a foreign word is a bad one, I resolved to spare anyone who had to read the poem aloud the affected mouthing. My second reason was that these cognomens usually give the reader or listener details about the characters which might be missed if attention were not drawn to them.

For the rest, almost any modern treatise or lecture on the art of translation since the Arnold-Newman controversy on the translation of Homer cleared the ground – and they seem to me to differ from each other in little but felicity of expression and aptness of example – will explain what I have tried to do.

ACKNOWLEDGEMENTS

In making this translation of *Sir Gawain and the Green Knight*, I have worked closely from the Early English Text Society's edition, edited by Sir Israel Gollancz, with introductory essays by Dr Mabel Day and Dr Mary Sergeantson, and compared it at all points with the edition of Professors J. R. R. Tolkien and E. V. Gordon. Dr Day has kindly allowed me to use some of the notes of the former edition and much of the material from her essay, for which I am most grateful. On the few occasions when I have followed Professor Tolkien, I have made separate acknowledgement. The prose translation by Mr Gwyn Jones, printed by the Golden Cockerel Press (which is very finely illustrated by Dorothea Braby), has often served as a check for the accuracy of the actual translation. In the compilation of the appendices, I used many books of reference, but especially the *Standard Dictionary of Folklore, Mythology and Legend*. I should like to thank the staff of the Reference Department of the Brighton Public Library for their help and interest.

To the friends on whose advice and criticism I have drawn, particularly Miss O. Alexander and Mr Seth Caine, I owe warm thanks. Mr Caine's erudition and sense of decorum have provided me with a sure touchstone at all times, and his encouragement has been worth much to me.

B. S.

Brighton, May 1958

Sir Gawain and the Green Knight[1]

PART ONE

I

THE siege and the assault being ceased at Troy,
The citadel smashed and smouldering in its ashes,
(The treacherous trickster[2] whose treasons there flourished
Was famed afar for malfeasance, falsehood unrivalled)
Aeneas the noble and his knightly kin
Then conquered kingdoms, and kept in their hand
Wellnigh all the wealth of the Western Isles.
Royal Romulus to Rome first turned
And built her battlements; abounding in pride,
He named her with his own name, which now she still has:
Ticius founded Tuscany, townships raising,
Longbeard in Lombardy lifted up homes,
And far over the French flood Felix Brutus[3]
Set Britain, on bluffs abundant and broad,
      In joy;

1. The manuscript bears no title, nor are the Parts or stanzas numbered.

2. Presumably Antenor who, when sent from Troy to negotiate with
Agamemnon, made a plan to deliver Troy and the Palladium to the Greeks.
At the fall of the city he was spared by the conquerors.

3. According to medieval legend, Brutus, the grandson of Aeneas, was the
founder of Britain. Geoffrey of Monmouth, in his *Historia Regum Britanniae*
(c. 1136), was possibly the first to make the suggestion.

Where war and woe and wonder
Their power often deploy,
And bliss and baneful blunder
By turns make man their toy.

II

AND when this Britain was built by this brave noble,
Here bold men bred, in battle exulting .
In turbulent times when trouble was rife.
Here many a marvel, more than in other lands,
Has befallen by fortune since that far time.
But of all who abode here of Britain's kings,
Arthur was highest in honour, as I have heard;
So an actual event here I aim to relate,
Which many folk mention as a manifest marvel,
A happening most eerie among Arthur's adventures.
Hearken to my history an hour or two:
Straightway shall I speak it, in city as I heard it,
          With tongue;
     As scribes have set it duly
     In the lore of the land so long,
     With letters linking truly
     In story bold and strong.

III

THIS king lay at Camelot one Christmastide
With loyal lords, liegemen peerless,
Members rightly reckoned of the Round Table,

In splendid celebration, seemly and carefree.
There tussling in tournament time and again
Jousted in jollity these gentle knights,
Then in court carnival sang catches and danced;
For there the feasting flowed for fully fifteen days
With all the meat and merry-making men could devise,
Gladly ringing glee, glorious to hear
Debonair rejoicing by day, dancing at night!
All was happiness in the height in halls and chambers
For lords and their ladies, delectable joy.
With all delights on earth they housed there together,
The most renowned knights acknowledging Christ,
The loveliest ladies to live in all time,
And the comeliest king ever to keep court.
For this goodly gathering was in its golden age
  Far famed,
  Well graced by God's good will,
  With its mettlesome king acclaimed:
  So hardy a host on hill
  Could not with ease be named.

IV

THE year being so young that yester-even saw its birth,
That day double on the dais were the diners served.
When the singing and psalms had ceased in the chapel,
The King and his company came into hall.
Called on with cries from clergy and laity,
Noël was newly announced, named time and again.
Then lords and ladies leaped forth, largesse distributing,

Granted New Year gifts graciously, gave them by hand,
Bustling and bantering about these offerings.
Ladies laughed full loudly, though losing their wealth,
And the winners were not woeful, you may well believe.
All this merriment they made until meal time.
Then in progress to their places they passed after washing,
In authorized order, the high-ranking first;
With glorious Guinevere, gay in the midst,
On the princely platform with its precious hangings
Of splendid silk at the sides, silk of Toulouse;
Turkestan tapestry toweringly canopied her,
Brilliantly embroidered with the best gems
Of warranted worth that wealth at any time
            Could buy.
      She gleamed, the most gracious dame,
      Glinting and grey of eye,
      That ever a knight could name;
      No rival with her could vie.

                              V

But Arthur would not eat until all were served.
He was charming and cheerful, child-like and gay,
And taking life lightly, little he loved
Lying down for long or lolling on a seat,
So robust his young brain and his beating blood.
Moreover, another matter moved him somewhat,
For he in noble style had announced he never would eat
On such a fair feast-day till informed in full

Of some unusual adventure, as yet untold,[1]
Of some momentous marvel that he might believe,
About ancestors, or arms, or other high theme;
Or till a stranger should seek out a strong knight of his,
To join with him in jousting, in jeopardy to lay
Life against life, each allowing the other
The favour of Fortune, the fairer lot.
Such was the King's custom when he kept court,
At all famous feasts among his free retinue
      In hall.
   So he throve amid the throng,
   A ruler royal and tall,
   Still standing staunch and strong –
   The year being young withal.

VI

ERECT stood the strong king, stately of mien,
Trifling time with talk before the topmost table.
Good Gawain was placed at Guinevere's side,
And Agravain of the Hard Hand[2] sat on the other side,
Both the King's sister's sons, staunchest of knights.
Above, Bishop Baldwin[3] began the board,

---

1. This custom is often referred to in medieval romances. Sometimes the adventure had to befall the court or some member of it; sometimes, as here, it was enough to have a report of it.

2. Agravain, Gawain's brother. Both were sons of King Lot of Orkney and Arthur's half-sister Anna (or Belisent).

3. Bishop Baldwin, the King's bishop and counsellor, sits in the place of honour nearest to the King.

And Ywain,[1] Urien's son, ate next to him.
These were disposed on the dais and with dignity served,
And many mighty men next, marshalled at side tables.
Then the first course came in with such cracking of trumpets,
(Whence bright bedecked blazons in banners hung)
Such din of drumming and a deal of fine piping,
Such wild warbles whelming in whirlpools of sound,
That hearts were uplifted high at the strains.
Then delicacies and dainties were delivered to the guests,
Fresh food in foison, such freight of full dishes
That space was scarce at the social tables
When the broth was brought in in bowls of silver
> To the cloth.
>> Each feaster made free with the fare,
>> Took lightly and nothing loth;
>> Twelve places were for every pair,
>> Good beer and bright wine both.

VII

OF their meal will I mention no more just now,
For all will acknowledge that ample was served.
At once another noise, a new fanfare, near at hand,
Gave the lords leave to lift food to their lips;
But barely had the blast of trump abated one minute
And the first course in the court been courteously served,
When there pressed in from the porch an appalling figure,
Who in height outstripped all earthly men.
From throat to thigh he was thickset and square;

1. Ywain, son of King Urien and Brimesent, another half-sister of Arthur's.

His loins and limbs were so long and great
That he was half a giant on earth, I believe,
Yet mainly and most of all a man he seemed,
And the handsomest of horsemen, though huge, at that;
For though at back and at breast his body was broad,
His hips and haunches were elegant and small,
And perfectly proportioned were all parts of the man,
     As seen.
   Amazed at the hue of him,
   A foe with furious mien,
   Men gaped, for the giant grim
   Was coloured a gorgeous green.

VIII

AND garments of green girt the fellow about –
A two-third length tunic, tight at the waist,
A comely cloak on top, accomplished with lining
Of the finest fur to be found, manifest to all,
Marvellous fur-trimmed material, with matching hood
Lying back from his locks and laid on his shoulders;
Fitly held-up hose, in hue the same green,
That was caught at the calf, with clinking spurs beneath
Of bright gold on bases of embroidered silk,
With shields for the shanks and shins when riding.
And verily his vesture was all vivid green,
So were the bars on his belt and the brilliants set
In ravishing array on his rich accoutrements.
It would be tedious to tell a tithe of the trifles
Embossed and embroidered, such as birds and flies,

In green gay and gaudy, with gold in the middle,
About himself and his saddle on silken work.
The breast-hangings of the horse, its haughty crupper,
The enamelled knobs and nails on its bridle,
And the stirrups that he stood on, were all stained with the same;
So were the saddle-bows and splendid tail-straps,
That ever glimmered and glinted with their green stones.
The steed that he spurred on was similar in hue

      To the sight,
  Green and huge of grain,
  Mettlesome in might
  And brusque with bit and rein –
  A steed to serve that knight!

IX

YES, garbed all in green was the gallant rider.
His hair, like his horse in hue, hung light,
Clustering in curls like a cloak round his shoulders,
And a great bushy beard on his breast flowing down,
With the lovely locks hanging loose from his head,
Was shorn below the shoulder, sheared right round,
So that half his arms were under the encircling hair,
Covered as by a king's cape, that closes at the neck.
The mane of that mighty horse, much like the beard,
Well crisped and combed, was copiously plaited
With twists of twining gold, twinkling in the green,
First a green gossamer, a golden one next.
His flowing tail and forelock followed suit,
And both were bound with bands of bright green,

Ornamented to the end with exquisite stones,
While a thong running thwart threaded on high
Many bright golden bells, burnished and ringing.
Such a horse, such a horseman, in the whole wide world
Was never seen or observed by those assembled before,

      Not one.
    Lightning-like he seemed
    And swift to strike and stun.
    His dreadful blows, men deemed,
    Once dealt, meant death was done.

X

YET hauberk and helmet had he none,
Nor plastron nor plate-armour proper to combat,
Nor shield for shoving, nor sharp spear for lunging;
But he held a holly cluster in one hand, holly[1]
That is greenest when groves are gaunt and bare,
And an axe in his other hand, huge and monstrous,
An axe fell and fearsome, fit for a fable;
For fully forty inches frowned the head.
Its handle-base was hued in green, in hammered gold and steel.
The blade was burnished bright, with a broad edge,
Acutely honed for cutting, as keenest razors are.
The grim man gripped it by its great strong handle,
Which was wound with iron all the way to the end,
And graven in green with graceful designs.

1. The holly cluster, or wassail bob, was a symbol of Christmas good luck, though its origin as such is wholly pagan. The early Christians in Rome probably took it over from the Saturnalia, in which it figured prominently.

A cord curved round it, caught at the head,
Then was hitched to the haft at intervals in loops,
With costly tassels attached thereto in plenty
On bosses of bright green embroidered richly.
In he rode, and up the hall, this man,
Pressing forward to the platform, no peril fearing.
He gave no one a greeting, but glared over all.
His opening utterance was, 'Who and where
Is the governor of this gathering? Gladly would I
Behold him with my eyes and have speech with him.'
      He frowned;
    He studied the standers-by
    And rolled his eyes around,
    Essaying to espy
    The noble most renowned.[1]

XI

THE assembled folk stared, long scanning the man,
For all men marvelled what it might mean
That a chevalier and charger should achieve such a hue
As to grow green as grass, and greener yet, it seemed,
More gaudily glowing than green enamel on gold.
The people pondered him, in perplexity neared him,
With all the world's wonder as to what he would do.
For astonishing sights they had seen, but such a one never;
Therefore a phantom from Fairyland the folk there deemed him.
So even the doughty were daunted and dared not reply,

1. The Green Knight evidently sees the place of honour empty, King Arthur having not yet taken his place.

All standing stock-still, astounded by his voice.
Throughout the high hall was a hush like death;
Quiet suddenly descended, as if sleep had stolen them
    To rest;
  For some were still for fear,
  And others at honour's behest;
  But let him whom all revere
  Greet that gruesome guest.

XII

FOR Arthur sensed an exploit before the high dais,
And accorded him courteous greeting, no craven he,
Saying to him, 'Sir knight, you are certainly welcome.
I am king of this castle; I am called Arthur.
Please deign to dismount and dwell with us
Till you impart your purpose, at a proper time.'
'May He that sits in heaven help me,' said the knight,
'But my intention was not to tarry in this turreted hall.
But as your reputation, royal sir, stands in rare honour,
And your castle and cavaliers are accounted the best,
Your men the most mettlesome in mounted combat,
The most warlike, the worthiest the world has bred,
Most valiant to vie with in virile contests,
And as chivalry is shewn here, so I am assured,
My bent has brought me here now, I am bound to declare.
By this branch that I bear, you may be certain
That I proceed in peace, no peril seeking;
For had I fared forth in fighting gear,
My hauberk and helmet, both at home now,

My shield and sharp spear, all shining bright,
And other weapons to wield, I would have brought;
However, as I wish for no war here, I wear soft clothes.
But if you are as bold as brave men affirm,
You will gladly grant me the good sport I demand
   By right.'
  Then Arthur said to him
  In answer: 'Noble knight,
  If deadly duel's your whim,
  We'll fail you not in fight.'

XIII

'No, it is not combat I crave, for come to that,
There are only beardless boys at this banqueting board.
If I were hasped in armour on a high steed,
No man among you could match me, your might being meagre.
Therefore in this court I crave a Christmas game,
For it is Yuletide and New Year, and young men abound here.
If any in this household is so hardy in spirit,
Of such mettlesome mind and so madly rash
As to strike a strong blow in return for another,
I shall offer to him this fine axe freely,
This axe, which is heavy enough, to handle as he please.
And I shall bide the first blow, as bare as I sit here.
If some intrepid man is tempted to try what I suggest,
Let him leap towards me and lay hold of this weapon,
Acquiring clear possession of it, no claim from me ensuing.
Then shall I stand up to his stroke, quite still on this floor –
So long as I shall have leave to launch a return blow
   Unchecked.

Yet he shall have a year
And a day's reprieve, I direct.
Now hasten and let me hear
Who answers, to what effect.'

XIV

IF he had astonished them at the start, yet stiller now
Were the henchmen in hall of every rank.
The rider wrenched himself round in his saddle
And wrathfully rolled his red eyes about,
Bending on all his brows, bristling and green,
His beard swaying as he strained to see who would rise.
When none came to accord with him, he coughed aloud,
And hemmed heavily before uttering this:
'What, is this Arthur's house, the honour of which
Is bruited abroad so abundantly?
Has your pride disappeared? Your prowess gone?
Your victories, your valour, your vaunts, where are they?
The revel and renown of the Round Table
Is now overwhelmed by a word from one man's voice,
For all flinch for fear from a fight not begun!'
Upon this, he laughed so loudly that the lord grieved.
His fair face and features were suffused with blood
        For shame.
    He raged as roaring gale;
    His followers felt the same.
    The King, not one to quail,
    To that cavalier then came.

35

XV

'By heaven,' then said Arthur, 'what you ask is foolish,
But as you firmly seek folly, find it you shall.
No good man here is aghast at your great words.
Hand me your axe now, for heaven's sake,
And I shall bestow the boon you bid us give.'
He leaped towards him lithely and laid hold of his hand,
And fiercely the other fellow footed the floor.
Now Arthur took his axe, holding the haft,
And swung it about sternly, as if to strike with it.
The bold man stood before him, big and tall,
Higher than any in the hall by a head and more.
He stroked his beard as he stood, stern of face,
Turning down his tunic in a tranquil manner,
Less unmanned and dismayed by the mighty strokes
Than if a banqueter at the bench had brought him a drink
      Of wine.
    Then Gawain at Guinevere's side
    Spoke to the King his design:
    'I beseech you fairly, confide
    This fight to me. May it be mine.

XVI

'If you would grant, great lord,' said Gawain to the King,
'That I might stir from this seat and stand beside you,
Be allowed without lese-majesty to leave the table,
And if my liege lady would likewise allow it,
I should come there to counsel you before this court of nobles.

For it appears unmeet to me, as manners go,
When your hall hears uttered such a haughty request,
For your great self to go forward and gratify it,
When on the benches about you so many bold men sit,
The best-willed in the world, as I well believe,
And the finest in the field when the fight is joined.
I am the most wanting in wisdom, and the weakest, I know,
And loss of my life would be least, in truth.
My only asset is that my uncle is my king;
There is no blessing in my body but what your blood accords.
And since this affair is so foolish that it should not fall to you,
And I first asked it of you, make it over to me;
And if I speak dishonourably, may all the court judge
     Without blame.'
    Then wisely they whispered of it,
    And after, all said the same:
    That the crowned king should be quit,
    And Gawain given the game.

XVII

THEN the King commanded the courtly knight to rise.
He directly uprose, made ready courteously,
Came to kneel to the King, and caught hold of the weapon.
Then Arthur happily handed it him
And gave him God's blessing, and gladly urged him
To be strong in spirit and stout of sinew.
'Cousin, take care with your one cut,' then counselled the King,
'And if you strike home successfully, surely then
You will stand the return stroke he will strike afterwards!'

Gawain goes to the man, great axe in hand,
And boldly and unabashed abides the outcome.
Then the man garbed in green said to Gawain the noble,
'Let us couch afresh our covenant, before we continue.
I constrain you, knightly sir, to state your name;
Tell it me truly and trustworthily.'
'In good faith,' said the good knight, 'Gawain is my name,
And whatever happens after, I offer you this blow,
And in twelve months' time I shall take the return
With whatever weapon you wish, and without seconds
            To strive.'
        The other with pledge replied,
        'I'm the merriest man alive
        It's a blow from you I must bide,
        Sir Gawain, so may I thrive.'

XVIII

'By God,' said the Green Knight, 'Sir Gawain, I rejoice
That I shall meet from your mailed fist my demand here.
And you have gladly gone over, in good discourse,
The covenant I requested of the King in full,
Except that you shall assent, swearing in truth,
To seek me yourself, in such place as you think
To find me under the firmament, and fetch your payment
For what you deal me today before this dignified gathering.'
'How shall I hunt for you? How find your home?'
Said Gawain. 'By God that made me, I go in ignorance;
Nor, knight, do I know your name or your court.
But instruct me truly thereof, and tell me your name,

And my utmost effort shall urge me thither,
So I offer you my oath, on my honour as a knight.'
'That is enough this New Year, no more is needed,'
Said the gallant in green to Gawain the courteous,
'To tell you the truth, when I have taken the blow
After you have duly dealt it, I shall directly inform you
About my house and my home and my own name.
Then you may keep your covenant, and inquire how I do,
And if I waft you no words, then well may you prosper,
Stay long in your own land and look for no further
      Trial.
   Now grip your weapon grim;
   Let us see your fighting style.'
   'Gladly,' said Gawain to him,
   Stroking the steel the while.

XIX

ON the ground the Green Knight graciously stood,
With head slightly slanting to expose the flesh.
His long and lovely locks he laid over his crown,
Neatly showing the naked neck, nape and all.
Gawain gripped his axe and gathered it on high,
Advanced the left foot before him on the ground,
And slashed swiftly down on the exposed part,
So that the sharp blade sheared through, shattering the bone,
Sank deep in the sleek flesh, split it in two,
And the scintillating steel struck the ground.
The fair head fell from the neck. On the floor it rolled,
So that people spurned and parried it as it passed their feet.

Then blood spurted from the body, bright against the green.
Yet the fellow did not fall, nor falter one whit,
But stoutly strode forward on legs still sturdy
To where the worthy knights stood, weirdly reached out,
Seized his splendid head and straightway lifted it.
Then he strode to his steed, snatched the bridle,
Stepped into the stirrup and swung aloft,
Holding his head by the hair in his hand.
He settled himself in the saddle as steadily
As if nothing had happened to him, though he had
     No head.
    He twisted his trunk about,
    That gruesome body that bled;
    He caused much dread and doubt
    By the time his say was said.

XX

FOR of a truth he held up the head in his hand,
Pointed the face at the fairest in fame[1] on the dais;
And it lifted its eyelids and looked glaringly,
And menacingly said with its mouth as you may now hear:
'Be prepared to perform what you promised, Gawain;
Seek faithfully till you find me, my fine fellow,
According to your oath in this hall in these knights' hearing.
Go to the Green Chapel without gainsaying to get
– And gladly will it be given in the gleaming New Year –
Such a stroke as you have struck. Strictly you deserve it.
As the Knight of the Green Chapel I am known to many;

1. That is, Guinevere.

Therefore if you ask for me, I shall be found.
So come, or else be called coward accordingly!'
Then he savagely swerved, sawing at the reins,
Rushed out at the hall door, his head in his hand,
And the flint-struck fire flew up from the hooves.
What place he departed to no person there knew,
Nor could any account be given of the country he had come from.
      What then?
   At the Green Knight Gawain and King
   Grinned and laughed again;
   But plainly approved the thing
   As a marvel in the world of men.

XXI

THOUGH honoured King Arthur was at heart astounded,
He let no sign of it be seen, but said clearly
To the comely queen in courtly speech,
'Do not be dismayed, dear lady, today:
Such cleverness comes well at Christmastide,
Like the playing of interludes, laughter and song,
And making fine music meet for lords and ladies.
However, I am now able to eat the repast,
Having seen, I must say, a sight to wonder at.'
He glanced at Sir Gawain, and graciously said,
'Now sir, hang up your axe: you have hewn enough.'
And on the backcloth above the dais it was boldly hung
Where all men might mark it and marvel at it
And with truthful testimony tell the wonder of it.
Then to the topmost table the two went together,

The King and the constant knight, and keen men served them
Double portions of each dainty in dignified style,
All manner of meat, and minstrelsy too.
Daylong they delighted till darkness came
        To their shores.
    Now Gawain, give a thought,
    For peril lest you pause,
    To seeking out the sport
    That you have claimed as yours.

PART TWO

I

Such was the earnest of adventures Arthur had at New Year,
For he was avid to hear of exploits by knights.
Though they had let fall few words when first seated,
Their loquacity knew no limit now, so lively was their talk.
Gawain was glad to begin the games in hall,
But though the end be heavy, have no wonder,
For if men are spritely in spirit after strong drink,
Soon the year slides past, never the same twice;
There is no foretelling its fulfilment from the start.
Yes, this Yuletide passed and the year following;
Season after season in succession went by.
After Christmas comes the crabbed Lenten time,
When fish and meagre fare are forced on the flesh.
Then weather more vernal wars with the wintry world,
The cold ebbs and declines, the clouds lift,
In shining showers the rain sheds warmth
And falls upon the fair plain, where flowers appear;
The grassy lawns and groves alike are garbed in green;
Birds prepare to build, and brightly sing
The solace of the ensuing summer that soothes hill
       And dell.
   By hedgerows rank and rich
   The blossoms bloom and swell,
   And sounds of sweetest pitch
   From lovely woodlands well.

II

THEN comes the season of summer with soft winds,
When Zephyrus himself breathes on seeds and herbs.
In paradise is the plant that springs in the open
When, the dew having dripped and dropped from the leaves,
It bears the blissful gleam of the bright sun.
Then Harvest comes hurrying, urging it on,
Warning it because of winter to wax ripe soon;
He drives the dust to rise with the drought he brings,
Forcing it to fly up from the face of the earth.
Wrathful winds in raging skies wrestle with the sun;
Leaves are lashed loose from the trees and lie on the ground,
And the grass becomes grey which was green before.
What rose from root and bud now ripens and rots;
So the year in passing yields its many yesterdays,
And winter returns, as the way of the world is,
     I swear;
    So came the Michaelmas moon,
    With winter threatening there,
    And Gawain considered soon
    The fell way he must fare.

III

YET he stayed in hall with Arthur till All Saints' Day,
When Arthur provided plentifully, especially for Gawain,
A rich feast and high revelry at the Round Table.
The gallant lords and gay ladies grieved for Gawain,

Anxious on his account; but all the same
They mentioned only matters of mirthful import,
Joylessly making jokes for that gentle man's sake.
For after dinner with drooping heart he addressed his uncle
And spoke plainly of his departure, putting it thus:
'Now, liege lord of my life, I beg my leave of you.
You know I must keep my covenant, I care for nothing else;
It would be trivial to tell you the trials thereof,
But I am bound to bear the blow and must be gone tomorrow
To seek the gallant in green, as God will direct me.'
Then the most courtly in that company came together,
Ywain and Eric[1] and others in troops,
Sir Dodinal the Fierce,[2] the Duke of Clarence,[3]
Lancelot[4] and Lionel[5] and Lucan the Good,[6]

1. Eric was well known from Chrétien de Troyes' Arthurian romances.

2. Sir Dodinal (or Doddinaval) 'le Savage' was so called on account of his love of hunting.

3. The Duke of Clarence, another cousin of Sir Gawain's, being the son of King Nantres and Arthur's half-sister Blasine, is particularly interesting because in the Vulgate 'Lancelot' he has an adventure similar to part of Gawain's. While looking for Gawain, who is imprisoned in the Dolorous Tower, he lodges with a vavasour who tries to dissuade him from travelling through a valley from which nobody returns. Even his squire tries to persuade him not to go on, and refuses to follow him into the valley.

4. Lancelot, the famous son of King Ban of Benwick, becomes an important figure only through the French romances. Later, as Queen Guinevere's lover, he becomes the chief knight of Arthur's court.

5. Lionel was the son of King Bohors of Gannes, and Lancelot's cousin.

6. Lucan, the royal butler, and Gifflet, in the Vulgate *Morte Arthur*, were the last left alive with Arthur after the final battle on Salisbury Plain. In the chapel Arthur, giving him a last embrace, pressed him to death.

Sir Bors[1] and Sir Bedivere,[2] both strong men,
And many admired knights, with Mador of the Gate.[3]
All this company of the court came near to the King
With carking care in their hearts, to counsel the knight.
There was much secret sorrow suffered in the hall
That such a gallant man as Gawain should go in quest
To suffer a savage blow, and his sword no more
          Should bear.
     Said Gawain, gay of cheer,
     'Whether fate be foul or fair,
     Why falter I or fear?
     What should man do but dare?'

IV

He dwelt there all that day, and at dawn on the morrow
Asked for his armour. Every item was brought.
First, the costly red carpet covering the floor
Was heaped with apparel and arms ornate with gold.
The strong man stepped on it, took the steel in hand.

1. Sir Bors was probably Lionel's brother.

2. Sir Bedivere, who in Malory and his source is the last survivor of Arthur's battle with Mordred, was the great friend of Sir Kay. Together they went with Arthur to meet the giant of St Michael's Mount, and later fought prodigiously in Arthur's great victory over the Romans. According to Geoffrey of Monmouth, both were slain in this battle.

3. Mador (de la Port), the brother of Gaheris de Careheu, was Arthur's chief porter. When Gaheris was killed at the Queen's table by poisoned apples intended for Gawain, Mador appealed for justice against the Queen. Guinevere could find no knight to defend her until, on the last of her forty days' respite, Sir Lancelot appeared in disguise and saved her life by defeating Mador.

The doublet he dressed in was dear Turkestan stuff.
Then came the courtly cape, cut with skill,
Finely lined with fur, and fastened close.
Then they set the steel shoes on the strong man's feet,
Lapped his legs in steel with lovely greaves,
Complete with knee-pieces, polished bright
And connecting at the knee with gold-knobbed hinges.
Then came the cuisses, which cunningly enclosed
His thighs thick of thew, and which thongs secured.
Next the hauberk, interlinked with argent steel rings
And resting on rich material, wrapped the warrior round.
He had polished armour on arms and elbows,
Glinting and gay, and gloves of metal,
And all the goodly gear to undergo what might
            Betide;
      With richly wrought surcoat
      And red-gold spurs to ride,
      And sword of noble note
      At his silken-girdled side.

                        V

WHEN he was hasped in armour his harness was noble;
The least lace or loop was lustrous with gold.
So, harnessed as he was, he heard his mass
And made offerings and orisons at the high altar.
Then he came to the King and his court-fellows,
Took leave with loving courtesy of lord and lady,
Who commended him to Christ and kissed him farewell.

By now Gringolet[1] had been got ready, and girt with a saddle
That gleamed most gaily with many golden fringes,
Everywhere nailed newly for this noble occasion.
The bridle was embossed and bound with bright gold;
So were the furnishings of the front armour and the fine skirts.
The crupper and the caparison accorded with the saddle-bows,
And all was arrayed on red cloth with nails of richest gold,
Which glittered and glanced like gleams of the sun.
Then he took hold of the helmet and hastily kissed it.
It was strongly stapled and stuffed with padding:
It towered high on his head and was hasped at the back,
And the visor was veiled by a vivid cover
Embroidered and bossed with the best gems
On broad silken borders, with birds on the seams,
Such as preening parrots, painted at intervals,
And turtles and true-love-knots traced as thickly
As if a score of maidens had been stitching it for seven winters
       In court.
    The circlet on his head
    Was thrice more precious thought
    And, perfectly diamonded,
    Sparkled in striking sort.

1. 'Gringolet' first appears in twelfth-century French as the name for a kind of
horse, though it may be from the Welsh 'Gwyngalet', meaning 'white-hard'.
But the name also belonged to the boat of the mythical hero Wade, the son of
Wayland the Smith and Bodhilda, the King of Sweden's daughter.

VI

THEN they showed him the shield with its shining gules,
With the Pentangle[1] in pure gold depicted thereon.
He brandished it by the baldric, and about his neck
He slung it in a seemly way, and it suited him well.
And I intend to tell you, though I tarry therefore,
Why the Pentangle pertains especially to this prince.
It is a symbol which Solomon conceived once
To betoken true faith, which it is entitled to,
For it is a figure which has five points,
And each line overlaps and is bound with another;
And it is endless everywhere, and the English call it,
As I have heard, the Endless Knot.
Therefore it goes with Sir Gawain and his gleaming armour,
For, ever faithful in five things, each in fivefold manner,
Gawain was known as a good man and, like gold well refined,
He was devoid of all villainy, every virtue displaying
            In the field.
    Thus this Pentangle new
    He carried on coat and shield,
    As a man of troth most true
    And knightly name annealed.

VII

FIRST he was found faultless in his five wits.
Next, his five fingers never failed the knight,
And all his trust on earth was in the five wounds

1. For the Pentangle, see Appendix Six.

Which came to Christ on the Cross, as the Creed tells.
And whenever the bold man was busy on the battlefield,
Through all other things he thought on this,
That his prowess all depended on the five pure Joys[1]
That the holy Queen of Heaven had of her Child.
Accordingly the courteous knight had that queen's image[2]
Etched on the inside of his armoured shield,
So that when he beheld her, his heart did not fail.
The fifth five I find the famous man practised
Were – Liberality and Lovingkindness leading the rest;
Then his Continence and Courtesy, which were never corrupted;
And Piety, the surpassing virtue. These pure five
Were more firmly fixed on that fine man
Than on any other, and every multiple,
Each interlocking with another, had no end,
Being fixed to five points which never failed,
Never assembling on one side, nor sundering either,
With no end at any angle; nor can I find
Where the design started or proceeded to its end.
Thus on his shining shield the shape of this knot
Was royally rendered in red gold on gules.
That is the pure Pentangle, so called by people wise
     In lore.
  Now Gawain was ready and gay;
  His splendid spear he bore,

1. The number of the joys may vary from five to fifteen. In medieval England they are usually five: the Annunciation, Nativity, Resurrection, Ascension, and Assumption.

2. It is usually Arthur who draws strength from the picture of the Virgin Mary etched on the inside of his shield.

And gave them all good day
As if for evermore.

VIII

HE struck the steed with his spurs and sprang on his way
So forcefully that the fire flew up from the flinty stones.
All who saw that seemly sight were sick at heart,
And all said to each other softly, in the same breath,
In care for that comely knight, 'By Christ, it is evil
That yon lord should be lost, who lives so nobly!
To find his fellow on earth, in faith, is not easy.
It would have been wiser to have worked more warily,
And to have dubbed the dear man a duke of the realm.
A magnificent master of men he might have been,
And so had a happier fate than to be utterly destroyed,
Beheaded by an unearthly being out of arrogance.
Who supposed the Prince would approve such counsel
As is giddily given in Christmas games by knights?'
Many were the watery tears that whelmed from weeping eyes,
When on quest that worthy knight went from the court
        That day.
    He faltered not nor feared,
    But quickly went his way:
    His road was rough and weird,
    Or so the stories say.

IX

Now the gallant Sir Gawain in God's name goes
Riding through the realm of Britain, no rapture in his mind.

Often at night he happened on neither house nor host,
Nor found placed before him the food that he liked –
He had no comrade but his courser in the country woods and hills,
No traveller to talk to on the track but God,
Till he was nearly nigh to Northern Wales.
The isles of Anglesey he kept always on his left,
And fared across the fords by the foreshore
Over at Holy Head[1] to the other side
Into the wilderness of Wirral,[2] where few dwelled
Who granted any good to God or man.
And always as he went, he asked whomever he met
If they knew or had knowledge of a knight in green,
Or could guide him to the ground where a green chapel stood.
And there was none but said him nay, for never in their lives
Had they set eyes on someone of such a hue

      As green.
   His way was wild and strange,
   By banks where none had been.
   His mood would many times change
   Before that fane was seen.

1. This place is clearly not in the position of modern Holyhead. It has been suggested that the ford across the Dee at Holywell is meant. There Caradoc, Prince of Wales, struck off St Winifred's head after she had refused his advances. Where the head fell, the holy well broke out. St Benno restored her to life, and the white circle round her neck remained as testimony of her fidelity to Christ. Sir Gawain would be interested in the mark on the neck.

2. In the fourteenth century the Wilderness of Wirral had become a refuge for vagabonds and outlaws to such an extent that in July 1376 Edward III, on the petition of the citizens of Chester, ordered the deforestation of the area.

X

HE rode far from his friends, a forsaken man,
Scaling many cliffs in country unknown.
At every bank or beach where the brave man crossed water,
He found a foe in front of him, except by a freak of chance,
And so foul and fierce a one that he was forced to fight.
So many marvels did the man meet in the mountains,
It would be too tedious to tell a tenth of them.
He had death-struggles with dragons, did battle with wolves,
Warred with wild trolls that dwelt among the crags,
Battled with bulls and bears and boars at other times,
And ogres that panted after him on the high fells.
Had he not been doughty in endurance and dutiful to God,
Certainly he had been slain and slaughtered many times.
Yet the warring little worried him; worse was the winter,
When the cold clear water cascaded from the clouds
And froze before it could fall to the fallow earth.
Half-slain by the sleet, he slept in his armour
Night after night among the naked rocks,
Where the cold streams ran clattering from the crests above
And hung high over his head in hard icicles.
So in peril and pain, in parlous plight,
This knight covered the country till Christmas Eve
          Alone;
     And he that eventide
     To Mary made his moan,
     And begged her be his guide
     Till some shelter should be shewn.

XI

MERRILY in the morning by a mountain he rode
Into a wondrously wild wood in a valley,
With high hills on each side overpeering a forest
Of huge heavy oaks, a hundred together.
The hazel and the hawthorn were intertwined,
And all was overgrown with hoar-frosted moss,
And on the bleak branches birds in misery
Piteously piped away, pinched with cold.
The gallant knight on Gringolet galloped under them
Through many a swamp and marsh, a man all alone,
Afraid of missing the functions of the feast day to come,
And not seeing the service of Him who that same night
Of a virgin was verily born to be victor over our strife.
And so, sighing, he said, 'I beseech thee, Lord,
And thee, Mary, mildest mother so dear,
That I may happen on some haven and there hear High Mass
And matins tomorrow morning: meekly I ask it,
And promptly thereto I pray my Pater and Ave
          And Creed.'
      He crossed himself and cried
      For his sins, and said, 'Christ speed
      My cause, His cross my guide!'
      So prayed he, spurring his steed.

XII

THRICE the sign of the Saviour on himself he had made,
When in the wood he was aware of a dwelling with a moat
On a promontory above a plateau, penned in by the boughs

And tremendous trunks of trees, and trenched about.
The comeliest castle ever acquired by a knight,
It was placed in an impregnable palisade
Of pointed stakes, on a plain with a park all round,
Containing many trees in its two-mile circumference.
The courteous knight contemplated the castle from one side
As it shimmered and shone through the shining oaks.
Then he heaved off his helmet and heartily thanked
Jesus and Saint Julian,[1] two gentle patrons
Who had given him grace and gratified his wish.
'Now grant it be good lodging!' the gallant knight said.
Then he goaded Gringolet with his golden heels,
And mostly by chance emerged on the main highway,
Which brought the brave man to the bridge's end
            With one cast.
       The drawbridge vertical,
       The gates shut firm and fast,
       The well-provided wall –
       It blenched at never a blast.

XIII

THE knight, still on his steed, stayed on the bank
Of the deep double ditch that drove round the place.[2]
Into the water the wall went wondrously deep,
And then to a huge height upwards it reared

1. Sir Gawain thanks St Julian as the patron saint of travellers.

2. The castle which the poet now proceeds to describe is of the highly ornamented kind introduced late in the fourteenth century. Possibly a building something like Caernarvon Castle was in his mind.

In hard hewn stone, up to the cornice,
Which was buttressed under the battlements in the best style
With protruding turrets between, equipped
With loopholes interlinked with lovely ornament.
No better barbican had ever been beheld by that knight,
And inside he could see a splendid high hall
With towers and turrets on top, all tipped with crenellations,
And pretty pinnacles placed along its length,
With carved copes, cunningly worked.
Many chalk-white chimneys the chevalier saw
On the tops of towers twinkling whitely –
And so many painted pinnacles disposed everywhere,
Congregated in clusters beyond the castle embrasures,
That it appeared like a prospect of paper patterning.
To the gallant knight on Gringolet it seemed good enough
If he could ever gain entrance to the inner court,
And harbour in that house while Holy Day lasted,
            Well cheered.
        He hailed, and at a height
        A civil porter appeared,
        Who welcomed the wandering knight,
        And his inquiry heard.

                            XIV

'Good sir,' said Gawain, 'will you give my message
To the high lord of this house, that I ask for lodging?'
'Yes, by Saint Peter,' replied the porter, 'and I think
You may lodge here as long as you like, sir knight.'
Then away he went, and swiftly returned

With a host of well-wishers to welcome the knight.
They let down the great drawbridge and in a dignified way
They came out and did honour to him by kneeling
On the cold ground courteously, according worthy welcome.
They granted passage through the gate, which gaped wide open,
And he reverently raised them and rode across the bridge.
Servitors held his saddle while he stepped down,
And his steed was stabled by strong men in plenty.
Then squires and knights descended ceremoniously
To bring the bold knight blithely into hall.
When he took off his helmet, many hurried forward
To receive it and to serve this stately man,
And his bright sword and buckler were both taken as well.
Then graciously he greeted each gallant knight,
And many proud men pressed forward to pay their respects.
Garbed in his fine garments, he was guided to the hall,
Where a fair fire on the hearth fiercely burned.
Then the prince of those people appeared from his chamber
To meet in mannerly style the man in his hall.
His first words were, 'You are welcome to dwell here:
Treat everything as your own, and have what you please
         In this place.'
    'I yield my best thanks yet:
    May Christ make good your grace!'
    Said Gawain and, gladly met,
    They clasped in close embrace.

XV

GAWAIN gazed at the gallant who had greeted him well
And it seemed to him the stronghold possessed a brave lord,
A powerful man in his prime, of stupendous size.
His beard of ruddy brown was broad and bright;
Stoutly he strode about on stalwart legs;
His face was fierce as fire, free was his speech,
And he seemed in good sooth a suitable man
To be prince of a people with companions of mettle.
This prince led him to an apartment and expressly commanded
That a man be commissioned to minister to Gawain;
And at his bidding a band of men bent to serve
Brought him to a beautiful room where the bedding was noble.
The bed-curtains, of brilliant silk with bright gold hems,
Had skilfully-sewn coverlets with comely panels,
And the fairest fur on the fringes was worked.
With ruddy gold rings on the cords ran the curtains;
Tapestry of Toulouse silk and Turkestan stuff
Furbished the walls and the floor underfoot as well.
There amid merry talk the man was disrobed,
And stripped of his battle-sark and his splendid clothes.
Retainers readily brought him rich robes
Of the choicest kind to choose from and change into.
Promptly he showed his preference and put on a robe
That sat on him in style, with spreading skirts.
And certainly it seemed spring-like to look on
To each knight who eyed all its hues;
And his lithe limbs below it showed lovely and glowing.
Jesus never made, so men judged, more gentle and handsome
          A knight:

From wherever in the world he were,
At sight it seemed he might
Be a prince without a peer
In field where fell men fight.

XVI

At the chimneyed hearth where charcoal burned, a chair was placed
For Sir Gawain in gracious style, gorgeously decked
With cushions on quilted work, both cunningly wrought;
And then a magnificent mantle, maroon in hue,
Of the finest fabric, and fur-lined with ermine,
As was the hood, was elegantly laid on him;
Perfect were the pelts, the most precious on earth.
In that splendid seat he sat in dignity,
And warmth came to him at once, bringing well-being.
Soon on trusty trestles a table was put up,
Then covered with a cloth shining clean and white,
And set with silver spoons, salt-cellars and napkins.
The worthy knight washed willingly, and went to his meat.
In seemly enough style servants brought him
Several fine soups, seasoned lavishly
Twice-fold, as is fitting, and fish of all kinds –
Some baked in bread, some browned on coals,
Some seethed, some stewed and savoured with spice,
But always subtly sauced, and so the man liked it.
The gentle knight generously judged it a feast,
And often said so, while the servers spurred him on thus
          As he ate:

'This present penance[1] do;
It soon shall be offset.'
The knight rejoiced anew,
For the wine his spirits whet.

XVII

THEN politely they put to that prince questions
In due form designed to draw him out,
So that he courteously conceded that he came of that court
Where high-souled Arthur held sway alone,
Ruler most royal of the Round Table;
And that Sir Gawain himself now sat in the house,
Having come that Christmas, by course of fortune.
Loudly laughed the lord when he learned what knight
He had in his house; such happiness it brought
That all the men within the moat made merry,
And promptly appeared in the presence of Gawain,
To whose person pertains all prowess and worth,
And pure and perfect manners, and praises unceasing.
His reputation rates first in the ranks of men.
Then each knight drew near to his neighbour and said,
Softly, 'Now shall we observe the seemliest manners
And faultless figures of virtuous discourse.
Without asking we may hear what utterance is lofty,
Since we have seized upon this scion of good breeding.

1. 'Penance'. As it is Christmas Eve, the fast day before the great feast begins, no meat is served, and hence the servers call the meal a penance, although Gawain, in recognition of the numerous ways in which the fish is presented, politely judges it to be a feast.

God has given us of his grace good measure,
In granting us such a guest as Gawain is,
When, contented at Christ's birth, the courtiers shall sit
      And sing.
   The manners of noble knights
   This baron to us shall bring.
   To his dalliance's delights
   Our listening souls shall spring.'

XVIII

WHEN the fine man had finished his food and risen,
It was nigh and near to the night's mid-hour.
Priests to their prayers paced their way
And rang the bells royally, as rightly they should,
To honour that high feast with evensong.
The lord inclines to prayer, the lady too;
Into her private pew she prettily walks;
Gawain advances gaily and goes there quickly,
But the lord gripped his gown and guided him to his seat,
Acknowledged him by name and benevolently said
In the whole world he was the most welcome of men.
Gawain spoke his gratitude, they gravely embraced,
And sat in serious mood the whole service through.
Then the lady had a longing to look on the knight;
With her bevy of beauties she abandoned her pew.
Most beautiful of body and bright of complexion,
Most winsome in ways of all women alive,
She seemed to Sir Gawain, excelling Guinevere.
To squire that splendid dame, he strode through the chancel.

Another lady led her by the left hand,
A matron, much older, past middle age,
Who was highly honoured by an escort of squires.
Most unlike to look on those ladies were,
For if the one was winsome, then withered was the other.
Hues rich and rubious were arrayed on the one,
Rough wrinkles on the other rutted the cheeks.
Kerchiefs with clear pearls clustering covered the one,
Whose breast and bright throat all bare appeared,
Shining like sheen of snow shed on the hills;
The other was swathed with a wimple wound to the throat
And choking her swarthy chin in chalk-white veils.
On her forehead were folded enveloping silks,
Trellised about with trefoils and tiny rings.
Nothing was bare on that beldame but the black brows,
The two eyes, protruding nose, and stark lips,
And those were a sorry sight and exceedingly bleary:
A grand lady, God knows, of greatness in the world
              Well tried!
        Her body was stumpy and squat,
        Her buttocks bulging and wide;
        More pleasure a man could plot
        With the sweet one at her side.

                        XIX

WHEN Gawain had gazed on that gracious creature,
He gained leave of the lord to go along with the ladies.
He saluted the senior, sweeping a low bow,
But briefly embraced the beautiful one,

Kissing her in courtly style and complimenting her.
They craved his acquaintance and he quickly requested
To be their faithful follower, if they would so favour him.
They took him between them, and talking, they led him
To a high room. By the hearth they earnestly demanded
Spices, which unstintingly men sped to bring,
And always with heart-warming, heady wine.
The lord often leaped lightly to his feet,
And many a time commanded that mirth should flow.
He took off his hood, hung it on a spear,
And offered it as a mark of honour to whoever should prove able
To make the most mirth that merry Yuletide.
'And I shall essay, I swear, to strive with the best
Before this garment goes from me, by my good friends' help.'
So with his mirth the mighty lord made things merry
To gladden Sir Gawain with games in hall
   That night;
  Until, the time being spent,
  The lord demanded light.
  Gawain took his leave and went
  To rest in rare delight.

XX

IN the morning, when men call to mind the birth
Of our dear Lord born to die for our destiny,
Ecstasy wells in all hearts for His sake:
And so it befell there on the feast day with fine fare.
Both at main meals and minor repasts strong men served
Rare dishes with fine dressings to the dais company.

Highest, in the place of honour, the ancient crone sat,
And the lord, so I believe, politely next.
Gawain and the gay beauty together in mid-table
Sat down in due order, as the dishes were served,
And thereafter throughout the hall, as was held best,
Graciously according to his degree, each gallant man was served.
There was meat and merry-making and much delight,
To such an extent that it would try me to tell of it;
And I suspect it would distract me to describe the details:
But yet I know the knight and the nobly pretty one
Found such solace and satisfaction seated together,
In their distinguished dalliance, their dignified talk,
Irreproachably pure and polished repartee,
That with the sport of princes their play of wit
      Compares.
    Pipes and side-drums sound,
    Trumpets entune their airs;
    Each soul its solace found,
    And the two were enthralled with theirs.

XXI

THAT day they made much merriment, and on the morrow again,
And thickly the joys thronged on the third day after;
But gentle was the jubilation on St John's Day,
The final one for feasting, so the folk there thought.
As there were guests geared to go in the grey dawn,
They watched the night out with wine, in wonderful style,
Leaping night-long in their lordly dances.
At last, when it was late, their leave-taking done,

They went their ways to dwellings far off.
Gawain also said good-bye, but the good host grasped him,
Led him to the hearth of his own chamber,
And held him back hard and highly thanked him
For the fine favour he had manifested to him
In honouring his house that high feast-tide,
And making his citadel splendid with his sparkling company:
'As long as I live, sir, my lustre shall be brighter
Now Gawain has been my guest at God's own feast.'
'Great thanks, sir,' said Gawain. 'In good faith, yours,
All yours is the honour, may the High King requite it!
I stand at your service, knight, to satisfy your will
As good use engages me, in great things and small,
          By right.'
     The prince then pressed in vain
     Longer to delay the knight,
     But Gawain urged again
     His departure in all despite.

XXII

THEN with courteous inquiry the castellan asked
What fierce exploit had sent him forth, at that festive season,
From the King's court at Camelot, so quickly and alone,
Before the holy time was over in the homes of men.
'You may, in truth, well demand,' admitted the knight.
'A high and urgent errand hastened me from thence,
For I myself am summoned to seek out a place
To find which I know not where in the world to look.

For all the land in Logres[1] – may our Lord help me! –
I would not fail to find it on the feast of New Year.
So this is my suit, sir, which I beseech of you here,
That you tell me in truth if tale ever reached you
Of the Green Chapel, or what ground or glebe it stands on,
Or of the knight who holds it, also coloured green.
For at that appointed place I am pledged, by the pact between us,
To meet that man, if I remain alive.
From now until the New Year is not a great time,
And if God will grant it me, more gladly would I see him
Than gain any good possession, by God's sun!
I must wend my way, with your good will, therefore;
I am reduced to three days in which to do my business,
And I think it fitter to fall dead than fail in my errand.'
Then the lord said laughingly, 'You may linger a while,
For I shall tell you where your tryst is by your term's end.
Give yourself no more grief for the Green Chapel's whereabouts,
For you may lie back in your bed, brave man, at ease
Till full morning on the First, and then fare forth
To the meeting-place at mid-morning, your mind to satisfy
            Out there.
        Leave not till New Year's Day,
        Then get up and go with cheer;
        You shall be shown the way;
        'Tis hardly two miles from here.'

1. Logres is generally taken to be the Kingdom of Arthur, or England south
of the Humber. Geoffrey of Monmouth derives its name from King Locrine,
just as our poet derives Lombardy from Longbeard (Longobardus) and Britain
from Brutus.

XXIII

THEN Gawain was glad and gleefully exclaimed,
'Now above all, most heartily do I offer you thanks!
For my goal is now gained, and by grace of yours
I shall dwell here and do what you deem good for me.'
Whereupon the prince, pressing his arm,
Sat beside him; then to solace them,
He let the ladies be fetched to delight them the more;
Set apart, they were transported in pleasures mutual,
And the lord, as one who was like to take leave of his senses,
And knew not what he would, uttered warm and merry words.
Then he spoke to Sir Gawain, saying out loud,
'You have determined to do the deed I ask:
Will you hold to your undertaking here and now?'
'Yes, sir, in good sooth,' said the true knight,
'While I stay in your stronghold, I shall stand at your command.
'Since you have spurred,' the lord said, 'from afar,
Then watched awake with me, you are not well supplied
With either sustenance or sleep, for certain, I know;
So you shall lie long in your room, late and at ease
Tomorrow till the time of mass, and then take your meal
When you will, with my wife beside you
To comfort you with her company till I come back to court.
        You stay,
    And I shall get up at dawn.
    I will to the hunt away.'
    When Gawain's agreement was sworn
    He bowed, as brave knights may.

XXIV

'MOREOVER,' said the man, 'Let us make a bargain
That whatever I win in the woods be yours,
And any achievement chancing to you be exchanged for it.
Sweet sir, truly swear to such a bartering,
Whether fair fortune or foul befall from it.'
'By God,' said the good Gawain, 'I agree to that,
And I am happy that you have an eye to sport.'
Then the prince of that people said, 'What pledge of wine
Is brought to seal the bargain?' And they burst out laughing.
They took drink and toyed in trifling talk,
These lords and ladies, as long as they liked,
And then in refined fashion, with many fair words,
They stood, softly speaking, to say good-night,
Kissing as they parted company in courtly style.
With lithe liege servants in plenty and lambent torches,
Each brave man was brought to his bed at last,
        Full soft.
    Before they fared to bed
    They rehearsed their bargain oft.
    That people's prince, men said,
    Could fly his wit aloft.

PART THREE

I

In the faint light before dawn folk were stirring;
Guests who had to go gave orders to their grooms,
Who busied themselves briskly with the beasts, saddling,
Trimming their tackle and tying on their luggage.
Arrayed for riding in the richest style,
Guests leaped on their mounts lightly, laid hold of their bridles,
And each rider rode out on his own chosen way.
The beloved lord of the land was not the last up,
Being arrayed for riding with his retinue in force.
He ate a sop hastily when he had heard mass,
And hurried with horn to the hunting field;
Before the sun's first rays fell on the earth,
On their high steeds were he and his knights.
Then these cunning hunters came to couple their hounds,
Cast open the kennel doors and called them out,
And blew on their bugles three bold notes.[1]
The hounds broke out barking, baying fiercely,
And when they went chasing, they were whipped back.
There were a hundred choice huntsmen there, whose fame
   Resounds.
  To their stations keepers strode;
  Huntsmen unleashed hounds:
  The forest overflowed
  With the strident bugle sounds.

1. The fourteenth-century hunting horn had only one note; a combination
of shorts and longs, like Morse code, was used for making different calls.

II

AT the first cry wild creatures quivered with dread.
The deer in distraction darted down to the dales
Or up to the high ground, but eagerly they were
Driven back by the beaters, who bellowed lustily.
They let the harts with high-branching heads have their freedom,
And the brave bucks, too, with their broad antlers,
For the noble prince had expressly prohibited
Meddling with male deer in the months of close season.[1]
But the hinds were held back with a 'Hey!' and a 'Whoa!'
And does driven with much din to the deep valleys.
Lo! the shimmering of the shafts as they were shot from bows!
An arrow flew forth at every forest turning,
The broad head biting on the brown flank.
They screamed as the blood streamed out, sank dead on the sward,
Always harried by hounds hard on their heels,
And the hurrying hunters' high horn notes.
Like the rending of ramped hills roared the din.
If one of the wild beasts slipped away from the archers
After being hunted from the high ground and harried to the water,
It was dragged down and met death at the dog-bases,
So skilled were the hunt-servants at stations lower down,
So gigantic the greyhounds that grabbed them in a flash,
Seizing them savagely, as swift, I swear,
        As sight.
    The lord, in humour high,
    Would spur, then stop and alight.
    In bliss the day went by
    Till dark drew on, and night.

1. In France, the close season was from 14th September to 3rd May.

III

THUS by the forest borders the brave lord sported,
And the good man Gawain, on his gay bed lying,
Lay hidden till the light of day gleamed on the walls,
Covered with fair canopy, the curtains drawn.
And as in slumber he slept on, there slipped into his mind
A slight, suspicious sound, and the door stealthily opened.
He raised up his head out of the bedclothes,
Caught up the corner of the curtain a little
And watched warily towards it, to see what it was.
It was the lady, loveliest to look upon,
Who secretly and silently secured the door,
Then bore towards his bed: the brave knight, embarrassed,
Lay flat with fine adroitness and feigned sleep.
Silently she stepped on, stole to his bed,
Caught up the curtain, crept within,
And seated herself softly on the side of the bed.
There she watched a long while, waiting for him to wake.
Slyly close this long while lay the knight,
Considering in his soul this circumstance,
Its sense and likely sequel, for it seemed marvellous.
'Still, it would be more circumspect,' he said to himself,
'To discover her desire straight away by speaking.'
So he stirred and stretched himself, twisting towards her,
Opened his eyes and acted as if astounded;
And, to seem the safer by such service, crossed himself
      In dread.
    With chin and cheek so fair,
    White ranged with rosy red,

With laughing lips, and air
Of love, she lightly said:

IV

'GOOD morning, Sir Gawain,' that gay lady said.
'How unsafely you sleep, that one may slip in here!
Now you are taken in a trice. But let a treaty be between us:
I shall bind you to your bed, of that be sure.'
The lady uttered laughingly those playful words.
'Good morning, gay lady,' Gawain blithely greeted her.
'Do with me as you will: that well pleases me.
For I surrender speedily and sue for grace,
Which, to my mind, since I must, is much the best course.'
And thus he repaid her with repartee and ready laughter.
'But if, lovely lady, your leave were forthcoming,
And you pleased to free your prisoner and pray him to rise,
I would abandon my bed for a better habiliment,
And have more happiness in our honey talk.'
'Nay, verily, fine sir,' urged the voice of that sweet one,
'You shall not budge from your bed. I have a better idea.
I shall hold you fast here on this other side as well,
And so chat on with the chevalier my chains have caught.
For I know well, my knight, that your name is Sir Gawain,
Whom all the world worships, wherever he ride;
For lords and their ladies, and all living folk,
Hold your honour in high esteem, and your courtesy.
And now – here you are truly, and we are utterly alone;
My lord and his liegemen are a long way off;
Others still bide in their beds, my bower-maidens too;

Shut fast and firmly with a fine hasp is the door;
And since I have in this house him who pleases all,
As long as my time lasts I shall lingering in talk take
     My fill.
    My young body is yours,
    Do with it what you will;
    My strong necessities force
    Me to be your servant still.'[1]

V

'In good sooth,' then said Gawain, 'Good luck is mine,
Though I am hardly the hero of whom you speak.
I am altogether unworthy, I own it freely,
To be held in such honour as you here suggest.
By God, I should be glad if you gave me leave
To essay, by speech or some other service,

1. This shameless avowal is of course contrary to the mode of wooing laid down in the canons of courtly love, and critics seem to have been at a loss to explain it. Sir Israel Gollancz's comment was: 'The Lady's bluntness in coming to the point testifies to her inexperience in such a role.' And Mr Gwyn Jones, in the introduction to his translation, writes of the Lady: 'She is an honest English rose.' This is to reduce her to an unwilling agent: I see her as an accomplished temptress, using every means short of magic – for a victory by magic could not succeed in its object of making Gawain sin. The Lady first hopes to catch the Knight off guard by a sudden assault. When this fails, she tries one trick after another from a repertory which draws on all the techniques of courtly love. Her ruthless lechery at the start is the one thing in her behaviour which, when the Green Knight makes his final revelation to Sir Gawain, satisfies the reader that she was an enchantress all the time, and not 'an honest English rose' temporarily pressed into service with the Faerie. And when we find familiars of Morgan the Fay in other romances similarly offering themselves, we are assured that our Lady fits the general pattern.

To pleasure such a perfect lady – pure joy it would be.'
'In good sooth, Sir Gawain,' the gay lady replied,
'If I slighted or set at naught your spotless fame
And your all-pleasing prowess, it would show poor breeding.
But there is no lack of ladies who would love, noble one,
Rather than have riches or the red gold they own,
To hold you in their arms, as I have you here,
And delight most lovingly in your light banter,
Which would perfectly pleasure them and appease their woes.
But as I love that Lord, the Celestial Ruler,
I have wholly in my hand what all desire

      Through His grace.'
   Not loth was she to allure,
   This lady fair of face;
   But the knight with speeches pure
   Answered in each case.

VI

'MADAM,' said the merry man, 'may Mary requite you!
For in good faith I have found in you free-hearted generosity.
Certain men for their deeds receive esteem from others,
But for myself, I do not deserve the respect they show me;
Your honour makes you aim only to speak well of me.'
'Now by Mary,' said the noble lady, 'not so it seems to me,
For were I worth the whole of womankind,
And all the wealth in the world were in my hand,
If I let myself look for a liege lord in marriage,
No lord that is living could be allowed to excel you,
With your fine virtues, knight, found by me here,

Your manly beauty, fair demeanour and meek courtesy,
All of which I had heard of before, but here have seen to be true.'
'I know for certain, noble lady,' the knight replied,
'Though I am proud of the precious price you put on me,
You selected a better lord. I lay at your feet
My service, and solemnly my sovereign I hold you.
I declare myself your cavalier, and may Christ repay you!'
Then of many matters they talked until mid-morn and after,
And all the time she behaved as if she adored him;
But Sir Gawain was on guard in a gracious manner.
Though she was the loveliest lady, yet less was the love
He could have for her; his imminent quest
      Decreed
   His destruction by the stroke
   Which he must have indeed.
   The lady of leaving then spoke;
   He gave his assent with speed.

VII

THEN she gave him good-bye, glinting with laughter,
And standing up, astounded him with these strong words:
'May He who prospers every speech for this pleasure reward you!
But scarcely a single soul would say you were Gawain.'
And the knight asked eagerly how this was so,
For he feared he had failed to observe the finest manners.
But the beauteous one blessed him and brought out this argument:
'Such a great man as Gawain is granted to be,
The very vessel of virtue and fine courtesy,
Could scarcely have stayed such a sojourn with a lady

Without craving a kiss in courtesy
At some point or pause in the pleasant talk.'
'So be it, as you say,' then said Gawain,
'I shall kiss at your command, as is becoming to a knight
Who fears to offend you; no further plea is needed.'
Whereupon she approached him, and penned him in her arms,
Leaned over him lovingly and gave the lord a kiss.
Then each commended the other to Christ in a comely manner,
And without more words she went out by the door.
He made ready to rise with rapid haste,
Summoned his servant, selected his garb,
And having dressed debonairly, walked down to mass.
And afterwards he ate in honourable style,
And made merry sport till the moon rose
       At night.
     Such welcome by women of name
     Was never given to knight,
     For the dear one and the dame
     Lavished on him delight.

VIII

AND still at his sport spurred the castellan,
Hunting the barren hinds in holt and on heath.
So many had he slain, by the setting of the sun,
Of does and other deer, that it was downright wonderful.
Then at the finish the folk flocked in eagerly,
And speedily piled the slain and slaughtered deer.
Those highest in rank came up with hosts of attendants,
Picked out the plumpest there, in the place of trial,

Where some were busy searching the assembled prey,
And had them opened honourably, as the task demands:
Two fingers' breadth of fat was found on the worst.
Then they slit open the slot, seized the second stomach,
Cut it away with a keen knife, and cleared it of flesh.
Next they hacked off all the legs, the hide was stripped,
The belly broken open and the bowels removed,
Carefully, lest they loosen the ligature of the knot.
Then they gripped the gullet, disengaged deftly
The wezand from the windpipe and whipped out the guts.
Then their sharp knives shore through the shoulder-bones,
Which they slid out of a small hole, leaving the sides intact.
Then they cleft the chest clean through, cutting it in two.
Then again at the gullet they began to work,
And rapidly rived it, right to the fork,
Flicked out the shoulder-fillets, and faithfully thereafter
They rapidly ripped free the rib-fillets.
Similarly, as is seemly, the spine was cleared
All the way to the haunch, which hung from it;
And they heaved up the whole haunch and hewed it off;
And that is named the numbles, in nature, or so
      I find.
    At the thigh-forks then they strain
    And free the folds behind,
    Hurrying to hack all in twain,
    The backbone to unbind.

IX

THEN they hewed off the head and also the neck,
And after sundered the sides swiftly from the chine,

And into the foliage they flung the fee of the raven.[1]
Then each fellow, for his fee, as it fell to him to have,
Skewered through the stout flanks beside the ribs,
And then by the hocks of the haunches they hung up their booty.
On one of the finest fells they fed their hounds,
And let them have the lights, the liver and the tripes,
With bread well imbrued with blood mixed with them.
Boldly they blew the kill amid the baying of hounds.
Then off they went homewards, holding their meat,
Stalwartly sounding many stout horn-calls.
As dark was descending, they were drawing near
To the comely castle where quietly our knight stayed.

     Fires roared,
  And blithely hearts were beating
  As into hall came the lord.
  When Gawain gave him greeting,
  Joy abounded at the board.

x

THEN the castellan commanded all to collect in hall,
And sent directions to the dames to come down with their maidens
Before all the folk on the floor, and further ordered
His venison to be fetched in front of him.
Then gaily and in good humour to Gawain he called,
Told over the tally of the sturdy beasts,
And showed him the fine fat flesh flayed from the ribs.
'How does the sport please you? Do you praise me for it?

1. The raven's fee. A piece of gristle on the end of the breast-bone or raven's
bone was always flung to the ravens and crows which gathered round a hunt.

Am I thoroughly thanked for thriving as a huntsman?'
'Certainly,' said the other. 'Such splendid spoils
Have I not seen for seven years, in the season of winter.'
'And I grant it you, Gawain, as a gift,' said the knight,
'For according to our covenant you may claim it as your own.'
'Certes, that is so, and I say the same to you,'
Said Gawain, 'for my true gains in this great house,
I am not loth to allow, must belong to you.'
And he put his arms round his handsome neck, hugging him,
And kissed him in the comeliest way he could think of.
'Accept my takings, sir, for I received no more;
Gladly would I grant them, however great they were.'
'And therefore I thank you,' the thane said. 'Good!
But better still would it be if you breathed in my ear
Where your wisdom won you wealth of that kind.'
'No such clause in our contract! Request nothing else!'
Said the other. 'You have your due: ask more,
            None should.'
        They laughed in blithe assent
        With worthy words and good;
        Then to sup they swiftly went,
        To fresh and dainty food.

XI

FINALLY by the fireside in a fair room they sat,
And chamberlains brought the chevaliers choice wines,
And in their jolly jesting they jointly agreed
On a settlement similar to the preceding one:
That on the next day, whatever happened to accrue

To each of them, it would be made over to the other man,
No matter how novel it was, at night when they met.
On this compact they closed, the whole court observing.
Then brave men brought forth the beverage to seal it,
And at last they lovingly took leave of each other,
Each man hastening thereafter to his bed.
The cock having crowed and called only thrice,
The lord leaped from bed, and his liegemen too,
So that mass and a meal were meetly dealt with,
And by first light the folk to the forest for the chase
            Were bound.
        With huntsman and with horns
        They go across the ground;
        Thrusting through the thorns,
        Unleashed runs every hound.

XII

By a quagmire they quickly scented quarry and gave tongue,
And the chief huntsman urged on the first hounds up,
Spurring them on with a splendid spate of words.[1]
The hounds, hearing it, hastened thither immediately,
Fell on the trail furiously, forty together,
And made such echoing uproar, all howling at once,
That the rocks round about rang with the din.
Hunters inspirited them with sound of speech and horn.

1. According to Turberville (*The Noble Art of Venerie, or Hunting*, 1573),
hounds engaged in boar-hunting needed special encouragement: 'You shall
comfort your houndes with furious terrible soundes and noyse, as well of the
voyce as also of your horne.'

Then together in a group, across the ground they surged
At speed between a pool and a spiked forest crag,
A great rugged rock which had roughly tumbled down
From the beetling cliff by the bogside.
They careered in full cry, with the courtiers after them.
Men surrounded the rugged rock and the morass as well,
Certain their prey skulked inside their ring,
For with the bloodhounds was the beast first to bay on the scent.
Then they beat upon the bushes and bade him come out,
And he swung out slanting, seeking the men,
A baneful boar of unbelievable size,
A solitary long since sundered from the herd,
Being old and brawny, the biggest of them all,
And grim and ghastly when he grunted: great was the grief
When he thrust through the hounds, hurling three to earth,
And sped on scot-free, swift and unscratched.
There were horn-calls and hallooing as the hounds were mustered,
And many were the merry cries from men and hounds
As they hurried clamouring after their quarry to kill him on
      The track.
   Many times he turns at bay
   And tears the dogs which attack.
   He hurts the hounds, and they
   Moan in a piteous pack.

XIII

THEN men shoved forward, shaped to shoot at him,
Loosed arrows at him, hitting him often
But the points, for all their power, could not pierce his flanks,

Nor would the barbs bite on his bristling brow,[1]
Though the smooth-shaven shaft shattered in pieces;
Yet wherever it hit, the head rebounded.
But when the boar was battered by blows unceasing,
Goaded and driven demented, he dashed at the men,
Striking them savagely as he assailed them in rushes,
So that some skulked away in stark fear.
But the lord on a lithe horse lunged after him,
Blew on his bugle like a bold knight in battle,
Rallied the hounds as he rode through the rank thickets,
Pursuing this savage boar till the sun set.
And so they disported themselves this day
While our lovable lord lay in his bed.
At home the gracious Gawain in gorgeous clothes
       Reclined:
    The gay one did not forget
    To come with welcome kind,
    And early him beset
    To make him change his mind.

XIV

SHE came to the curtain and cast her eye
On Sir Gawain, who at once gave her gracious welcome,
And she answered him eagerly, with ardent words,
Sat down softly at his side, and with swift laughter
And a languishing look, delivered these words:

1. The bristles of the brow grow thicker when the boar has its winter coat.
When at bay, with its flanks and rear protected, the boar could be fatally hit
only by a shot between the eyes.

'It seems to me strange if, sir, you are Gawain,
One who is always so apt to show virtue,
Yet does not know at all the nicest manners,
And if anyone instructs you in them, you ignore them.
Quickly you have cast away what I schooled you in yesterday
By the truest of all tokens of talk I know of.'
'What?' said the wondering knight, 'I am not aware of one.
But if it be true what you tell, I am entirely to blame.'
'Yet I counselled you about kissing,' the comely one said;
'Where a favour is conferred, it must firmly be claimed
According to the canons of courtly usage.'
'Sweet one, unsay that speech,' said the brave man,
'For I dared not do that lest I be denied.
If I made advances and were refused, I should be found at fault.'
'By my faith,' said the bright lady, 'none could rebuff you.
You are strong enough to constrain one with your strength if you wish,
If any were so unmannerly as to offer you resistance.'
'Yes, you have given me good advice, by God,' replied Gawain,
'But threateners are ill thought of and do not thrive in my country,
Nor do gifts thrive when given without good will.
I am here at your behest, to offer a kiss to when you like;
You may do it whenever you deem fit, or desist,
             In this place.'
       The beautiful lady bent
       And fairly kissed his face:
       Much speech the two then spent
       On love, its grief and grace.

XV

'IF it did not anger you,' the high-born lady said,
'I would ask you why it is that one so young,
So hale and hearty as you are at this time,
So generous a gentleman as you are justly known to be,
Has never uttered any word that I have hearkened to
Belonging to love's saga, neither less nor more.[1]
The choicest thing in Chivalry, the chief thing praised,
Is the loyal sport of love, the very lore of arms;
The tale of the contentions of the true knights
Is told by the title and text of their works –
How lords for their true loves put their lives at hazard,
Endured dreadful trials for their dear loves' sakes,
And with their valour took revenge for their vicissitudes,
And brought home abundant bliss by their virtues.
You are the gentlest and most just of your generation:
Everywhere your honour and high fame are known.
And two separate times I have sat beside you here.
Being so polished and so punctilious a pledge-fulfiller,
You ought to be eager to indicate to a young lady
And discover the high craft of courtly love.
Why! Are you ignorant, you who have all the fame?
Or do you deem me too dull to delight in your dalliance?
         For shame!

1. The text breaks off after the fourth line of the stanza, and a lengthy paren
thesis follows: yet the original sentence is never properly resumed. To resolv
the difficulty and produce a consecutive translation, I have taken lines 1523–
and placed them at the beginning of what is the parenthesis in the original
This is the only place in the poem where I have seriously tampered with th
order of the original.

I came here single, and sit
With you to fan love's flame.
Open my eyes to your wit,
While my husband is out hunting game.'

XVI

IN good faith,' said Gawain, 'may God requite you!
It gives me great happiness, and is good sport to me,
That so fine a fair one as you should find her way here
And take pains with so poor a man, make pastime with her knight,
With any kind of clemency – it comforts me greatly.
But in faith it would be a manifold folly, noble lady,
For me to take on the travail of interpreting true love
And construing the subjects of the stories of arms
To you who, I hold, have more skill
In that art, by half, than a hundred of such
As I am or ever shall be on the earth I inhabit.
To please you I would press with all the power in my soul,
For I am highly beholden to you, and evermore shall be
True servant to your bounteous self, so save me God!'
So the stately lady tempted him and tried him with questions
To persuade him to sin, with some other motive besides.[1]
But he defended himself so firmly that no fault appeared,
Nor was there any evil apparent on either side,
          But bliss;
     For long they laughed and played
     Till she gave him a gracious kiss.

1. This is the poet's first hint that the Lady is not concerned solely with the gratification of her desire.

A fond farewell she bade,
And went her way on this.

XVII

THEN Gawain dons his garments and goes to mass:
Next, dinner is daintily dressed and served.
All day long the lord and the ladies disported,
But the castellan often coursed across the country,
Pursued his savage boar, which swooped over the slopes,
And bit asunder the backs of his best hounds
When at bay, till the bowmen obliged him to break free,
And forced him, for all his defence, to go farther away,
So fast the arrows flew when the folk concentrated.
Sometimes he made even the strongest start back.
In time he became so tired he could tear away no more,
But with the speed he still possessed, he spurted to a hole
On a rise by a rock with a running stream beside.
He got the bank at his back, and began to abrade the ground.
The froth was foaming foully at his mouth,
And he whetted his white tusks; a weary time it was
For the bold men about, who were bound to harass him
From a distance, for none dared to draw near him
            For dread.
        He had hurt so many men
        That it entered no one's head
        To be torn by his tusks again,
        And he raging and seeing red.[1]

[1.] I am afraid people with Yeats in their blood must be permitted this kind of construction.

XVIII

TILL the castellan came himself, encouraging his horse,
And saw the boar at bay with his band of men around.
He alighted in lively fashion, left his courser,
Drew and brandished his bright sword and boldly strode forward,
Striding at speed through the stream to where the savage beast was.
The wild thing was aware of the weapon and its wielder,
And bridled with his bristles in a burst of fierce snorts,
So that all were anxious for the lord, lest worst hap befall.
Straightaway the swine sprang out at the man,
And baron and boar were both in a heap
In the swirling water: the worst went to the beast,
For the man had marked him well at the moment of impact,
Had put the point precisely at the pit of his chest,
And drove it in to the hilt, so that the heart was shattered,
And the spent beast sank snarling in the stream,
          Teeth bare.
    A hundred hounds and more
    Attack and seize and tear;
    Men tug him to the shore
    And the dogs destroy him there.

XIX

BUGLES blew the triumph, horns blared loud.
There was hallooing on high by all those present;
Braches bayed their best at the bidding of their masters,
The chief huntsmen in charge of that chase so hard.
Then one who was wise in wood-crafts
Started in style to slash open the boar.

First he hewed off the head and hoisted it on high,
Then rent him roughly along the ridge of his back,
Brought out the bowels and broiled them on coals
For blending with bread as the braches' reward.
Then he broke out the brawn from the bright broad flanks,
And heaved out the entrails, as honour requires,
Attached the two halves entirely together,
And on a strong stake stoutly hung them.
Then with this same swine they started for home.
With the boar's head borne before the baron himself,[1]
Who had destroyed him in the stream by the strength of his arm,
          Above all:
      It seemed to him an age
      Till he greeted Gawain in hall.
      To reap his rightful wage
      The latter came at his call.

                              XX

THE lord exclaimed loudly, laughing merrily
When he saw Sir Gawain, and spoke joyously.
The sweet ladies were sent for, and the servants assembled.
Then he showed them the shields, gave a short account
Of the large size, the length, the malignity
And fighting style of the fierce boar when he fled in the woods;

1. The Boar's Head Carol reminds us of the association of boar-hunting with
Christmas, but according to the forest laws, the boar-hunting season began
only on Christmas Day, so that an early kill was vital if the board was to be
properly graced for the evening meal. Candlemas, 2nd February, marked the
end of the boar-hunting season.

So that Gawain congratulated him on his great deed,
Commended it as a merit he had manifested well.
For such a brawny beast, the bold man said,
A boar of such breadth, he had not before seen.
When they handled the huge head the upright man praised it,
Expressed horror thereat for the ear of the lord.
'Now Gawain,' said the good man, 'this game is your own
By our contracted treaty, in truth, you know.'
'It is so,' said the knight, 'and as certainly
I shall give you all my gains as guerdon, in faith.'
He clasped the castellan's neck and kissed him kindly,
And then served him a second time in the same style.
'In all our transactions since I came to sojourn,' asserted Gawain,
'Up to tonight, as of now, there's nothing that
        I owe.'
    'By Saint Giles,'¹ the castellan quipped,
    'You're the finest fellow I know:
    Your wealth will have us all whipped
    If your trade continues so!'

XXI

THEN the trestles and tables were trimly set out,
Complete with cloths, and clearly-flaming cressets
And waxen torches were placed in the wall-brackets

---

1. St Giles was a seventh-century hermit who, persecuted by fame, withdrew
to a forest near Nîmes, where he lived with a hind as his sole companion. This
hind, when hunted by the king, led him to St Giles, whom the king persuaded
to build a Benedictine monastery. The attribute of the hind makes this saint a
most suitable patron for Sir Bertilak.

By retainers, who then tended the entire hall-gathering.
Then by the fire on the floor, in multifarious ways
A spirit of gladness and glee gushed forth,
And many songs[1] were sung at supper and afterwards,
A concert of Christmas carols[1] new and old,
With the most mannerly mirth a man could tell of.
And our courteous knight kept constant company with the lady.
In a bewitchingly well-mannered way she ogled him,
Surreptitiously soliciting the stalwart knight,
So much so that he was astounded, and upset in himself.
But his upbringing forbade him to oblige her,
And he dealt with her daintily – a deed not tending to
        Disgrace.
    As long as they like in hall
    In glee they play with grace,
    And then at the castellan's call
    To the chimney-piece they pace.

XXII

THERE they drank and discoursed and decided to enjoy
Similar solace and sport on New Year's Eve.
But the princely knight asked permission to depart in the morning,
For his appointed time was approaching, and perforce he must go.
But the lord would not let him and implored him to linger,
Saying, 'I swear to you, as a staunch true knight,
You shall gain the Green Chapel to give your dues,

1. In the original, two kinds of sung music are specified. One is the 'conduit',
a Christmas song for tenor with two descants, and the ancestor of the modern
carol. The other is the 'carole', the dancing song of the Middle Ages.

My lord, in the light of New Year, long before sunrise.
Therefore remain in your room and rest in comfort,
While I fare hunting in the forest; in fulfilment of our oath
Exchanging what we achieve when the chase is over.
For twice I have tested you, and twice found you true.
Now may you thrive best the third time! Think of the morrow.
Let us make merry while we may, set our minds on joy,
For disaster can seize man whensoever it pleases.'
This was graciously granted and Gawain stayed.
Bright wine was gladly brought them and then to bed they went
      With light.
    Sir Gawain lies and sleeps
    Softly and still all night,
    But the lord his custom keeps
    And is early up and dight.

XXIII

MERRY was the morning, and mass being said,
After a small meal he bespoke his saddle-horse;
The men were ready mounted before the main gate,
A host of knightly horsemen to follow after him.
Wonderfully fair was the forest-land, for the frost remained,
And the rising sun shone ruddily on the ragged clouds,
In its beauty brushing their blackness off the heavens.
The huntsmen uncoupled the hounds by a forest,
And the rocks resounded with their ringing horns.
Some found the fox's[1] tracks and fared forward,

1. Although accounts of the hunting of deer and boar are common in medieval
romance, descriptions of fox-hunting are rare.

Weaving across various ways in their wily fashion.
A small hound cried the scent, the senior huntsman called
His fellow foxhounds to him and, feverishly sniffing,[1]
The rout of dogs rushed forward on the right path.
The fox hurried fast, for they found him soon
And, seeing him distinctly, pursued him at speed,
Unmistakably giving tongue with tumultuous din.
Deviously in difficult country he doubled on his tracks,
Swerved and wheeled away, often waited listening,
Till at last by a little ditch he leaped a quickset hedge,
And stole out stealthily at the side of a valley,
Considering his stratagem had given the slip to the hounds.
Then he stumbled on a tracking-dogs' tryst-place unawares,
And there in a cleft three hounds threatened him at once,

> All grey.
> He swiftly started back
> And, full of deep dismay,
> He dashed on a different track;
> To the woods he went away.

XXIV

THEN came the lively delight of listening to the hounds.
When they had all met in a muster, mingling together,
In their crying they called down such curses upon him
That the clustering cliffs seemed to be crashing down.
Here he was hallooed when the hunters met him,
There savagely snarled at by intercepting hounds;

1. Turberville recommends the putting of vinegar into the nostrils of a hound 'for to make him snuffe, to the end his sent may be the perfecter'!

Then he was called thief and threatened often;
With the tracking dogs on his tail, no tarrying was possible.
Out into the open they often chased him;
But so wily Reynard was, that he wheeled back again.
So he led the lord and his liegemen a dance
In this manner among the mountains till mid-morning,
While harmoniously at home the honoured knight slept
Between the comely curtains in the cold morning.
But the lady would not let herself sleep for love,
Nor would she impair the purpose pitched in her heart,
But rose up rapidly and ran to him
In a ravishing robe that reached to the ground,
Trimmed with finest fur from pure pelts,
Her head not conventionally coifed, costly stones
Being strung in scores on her splendid hairnet.
Her well-favoured face and fair throat were exposed,
Her breast was bare and her back as well.[1]
She came in by the chamber door and closed it after her,
Cast open a casement and called on the knight,
Cheerfully chiding him with her chivalrous words,

      As beseems:
  'Ah, sir! How sound you sleep!
  Bright are the morning's beams.'
  He was drowsing deep,
  But her banter broke his dreams.

1. In her extreme décolletage, the Lady is using a standard weapon in the love
wars of *amour courtois*.

XXV

THE noble sighed ceaselessly in unsettled slumber
As threatening thoughts thronged in the dawn light
About destiny, which the day after would deal him his fate
At the Green Chapel where Gawain was to greet his man,
And was bound to bear his buffet unresisting.
But having recovered consciousness in comely fashion,
He heaved himself out of dreams and answered hurriedly.
The lovely lady advanced, laughing adorably,
Swooped over his splendid face and sweetly kissed him.
He welcomed her worthily with noble cheer
And, gazing on her gay and glorious attire,
Her features so faultless and fine of complexion,
He felt a flush of rapture suffuse his heart.
Sweet and genial smiling slid them into joy
Till bliss burst forth between them, beaming gay
              And bright;
       Ecstatically they contend
       In talk of true delight
       Till dangerous passions impend –
       But Mary minded her knight.

XXVI

FOR that peerless princess pressed him so hotly,
So invited him to the very verge, that he felt forced
Either to allow her love or blackguardly rebuff her.
He was concerned for his courtesy, lest he be called caitiff,
But more especially for his evil plight if he should plunge into sin,
And dishonour the owner of the house treacherously.

'God shield me! That shall not happen, for sure,' said the knight.
So with laughing love-talk he deflected gently
The downright declarations that dropped from her lips.
Then said the sweet one to Sir Gawain,
'You deserve more censure than any servant of love alive
If you love not the living body lying close to you;
Unless you have a lover more beloved, whom you like better,
A maiden to whom you are committed, so immutably bound
That you do not seek to sever from her – which I see is so.
Tell me the truth of it, I entreat you now;
By all the loves there are, do not hide the truth
      With guile.'
    Then gently, 'By Saint John,'
    Said the knight with a smile,
    'I owe my oath to none,
    Nor wish to yet a while.'

XXVII

'THOSE words,' said the fair woman, 'are the worst there could be,
But I am truly answered, to my utter anguish.
Give me now a gracious kiss, and I shall go from here
As a maid that loves much, mourning on this earth.'
Then, sighing, she stooped, and seemlily kissed him,
And, severing herself from him, stood up and said,
'At this adieu, my dear one, do me this pleasure:
Give me something as your gift, your glove perhaps,
To mitigate my mourning when I remember you.'
'Now certainly, for your sake,' said the knight,
'I wish I had here the handsomest thing I own,

For you have deserved, forsooth, superabundantly
And rightfully, a richer reward than I could give.
But as tokens of true love, trifles mean little.
It is not to your honour to have at this time
A mere glove as Gawain's gift to treasure.
For I am here on an errand in unknown regions,
And have no bondsmen, no baggages with dear-bought things in them.
This afflicts me now, fair lady, for your sake.
But we are bound by Fate and must bravely bear its
   Decree.'
  'No, highly honoured one;
  (The gay one would not agree)
  Though gift you give me none,
  Yet take this token from me.'

XXVIII

SHE proffered him a rich ring wrought in red gold,
With a sparkling stone set conspicuously in it,
Which beamed as brilliantly as the bright sun;
You may well believe its worth was wonderfully great.
But the courteous man declined it and quickly said,
'Before God, my gay one, no giving just now!
Not having anything to offer, I shall accept nothing.'
She offered it him urgently and he refused again,
Fast affirming his refusal on his faith as a knight.
Put out by this repulse, she presently said,
'If you reject my ring as too rich in value,
Doubtless you would be less deeply indebted to me
If I gave you my girdle, a less gainful gift.'

She gracefully grasped the girdle of her gown
Which went round her waist under the wonderful mantle,
A girdle of green silk with a golden hem
Embroidered only at the edges, with hand-stitched ornament.
And she pleaded with the prince in a pleasant manner,
But he told her that he could touch no treasure at all,
Not gold nor any gift, till God gave him grace
To pursue to success the search he was bound on.
'So I entreat you to be contented, therefore,
And press no more your purpose, for I promise it never
        Can be.
    I am deep in debt to you, dame,
    Because of your manner to me,
    And ever through ice and flame
    I shall stay your devotee.'

XXIX

'Do you say "no" to this silk?' then said the beauty;
'In itself such a simple-seeming thing?
And lo! Being little, it has less value.
But one who was aware of the worth twined in it
Would appraise its properties as more precious perhaps,[1]
For the man that binds his body with this belt of green,
As long as it is lapped closely about him,
Is safe from assailants, whoever strives to slay him,

1. The magic girdle is naturally found elsewhere in medieval romance. In
Diu Krône, Gawain gives to Guinevere, who in turn gives to Gasozein, a girdle
which makes the wearer invincible in battle and brings him the love of men
and women.

For he cannot be killed by any cunning there is.'
Then the prince pondered, and it appeared to him
It would protect him in the peril appointed to him
When he gained the Green Chapel to be given checkmate:
It would be a splendid stratagem to escape being slain.
Then he allowed her to solicit him and let her speak.
She pressed the belt upon him with potent words
And gladly gave it him when he agreed to accept it,
Beseeching him for her sake to conceal it always,
And hide it from her husband with all diligence.
That never should another know of it, the noble pledged
          His plight.
     Then often his thanks gave he
     With all his heart and might,
     And thrice by then had she
     Kissed the constant knight.

          xxx

THEN with a word of farewell she went from him,
For further satisfaction was not forthcoming.
Directly she had departed, Sir Gawain dressed himself,
Rose and arrayed himself in rich garments,
But laid aside the love-lace the lady had given him,
Secreted it carefully where he could discover it later.
Then he wended his way at once to the chapel,
Privily approached a priest and prayed him there
To uplift him in his life and enlighten him
On how he might have salvation in the hereafter.

Then, confessing his faults, he fairly shrove himself,[1]
Begging mercy for both major and minor sins.
He asked the holy man for absolution
And was absolved with certainty and sent out so pure
That Doomsday should have been declared the day after.
Then he made merrier among the noble ladies,
With comely carolling and all kinds of pleasure,
Than ever he had done, with ecstasy,
      Till night.
    Such honour he did to all,
    They said, 'Never has this knight
    Since coming into hall
    Expressed such pure delight.'

XXXI

Now long may he linger there, love sheltering him!
The prince was still on the plain, pleasuring in the chase,
Having finished off the fox he had followed so far.
As, looking out for the evil fox, he leaped over a hedge
Where he heard the hounds that were harrying him,
Reynard came rushing through a rough thicket,
With the whole pack pell-mell after, panting at his heels.
The lord, aware of the wild beast, waited craftily

---

1. It is a flaw in the Christian purity of the poem that Gawain is allowed to
make a full confession and yet retain the use of the girdle. It is difficult to argue
that this sacrilege is part of the sin later punished by the Green Knight; which
leaves us with the unpleasant proposition that this is either a technical or a
theological oversight on the part of the poet. Perhaps he thinks Sir Gawain
justified by the 'necessity' mentioned in line 2040 on page 105, but even that
does not excuse the sacrilege.

And drew his dazzling sword and drove at the fox.
The beast baulked at the blade to break sideways,
But a dog bounded at him before he could,
And right in front of the horse's feet they fell on him,
All worrying their wily prey with a wild uproar.
The lord quickly alighted and lifted him up,
Raised him beyond reach of the ravening fangs,
Held him high over his head and hallooed lustily,
While the angry hounds in hordes bayed at him.
Thither hurried the huntsmen with horns in plenty,
Sounding the rally splendidly till they saw their lord.
When the company of his court had come up to the kill,
All who bore bugles blew at once,
And the others without horns hallooed loudly.
The requiem that was raised for Reynard's soul
And the commotion made it the merriest meet ever,
      Men said.
    The hounds must have their fee:
    They pat them on the head,
    Then hold the fox; and he
    Is reft of his skin of red.

XXXII

THEN they set off for home, it being almost night,
Blowing their big horns bravely as they went.
At last the lord alighted at his beloved castle
And found upon the floor a fire, and beside it
The good Sir Gawain in a glad humour
By reason of the rich friendship he had reaped from the ladies.

He wore a turquoise tunic extending to the ground;
His softly-furred surcoat suited him well,
And his hood of the same hue hung from his shoulder.
All trimmed with ermine were hood and surcoat.
Meeting the master in the middle of the floor,
Gawain went forward gladly and greeted him thus:
'Forthwith, I shall be the first to fulfil the contract
We settled so suitably without sparing the wine.'
Then he clasped the castellan and kissed him thrice
As sweetly and steadily as a strong knight could.
'By Christ!' quoth the other. 'You will carve yourself a fortune
By traffic in this trade when the terms suit you!'
'Do not chop logic about the exchange,' chipped in Gawain,
'As I have properly paid over the profit I made.'
'Marry,' said the other man, 'mine is yet to pay,
For I have hunted all day and have only taken
This ill-favoured fox's skin, may the Fiend take it!
And that is a poor price to pay for such precious things
As you have pressed upon me here, three pure kisses
        So good.'
    'Enough!' acknowledged Gawain,
    'I thank you, by the Rood.'
    And how the fox was slain
    The lord told him as they stood.

XXXIII

THEN they made as merry as any men may,
With minstrelsy and mirth, and meals at their will,
With the laughter of ladies and delightful jesting.

Very glad then together were Gawain and the host,
Save when excess or sottishness seemed likely.
Many jests were made by master and men,
Until presently, at the appointed parting-time,
All men at last had to go up to bed.
Then of his host the honoured man humbly took his leave,
Giving him gracious thanks, being greatly indebted:
'May the High King requite you for your courtesy at this feast,
And the wonderful week of my dwelling here!
I would offer to be one of your own men if you liked,
But that I must move on tomorrow, as you know,
If you will give me the guide you granted me,
To show me the Green Chapel where my share of doom
Will be dealt on New Year's Day, as God deems for me.'
'With all my heart!' said the host. 'In good faith,
All that I ever promised you, I shall perform.'
He assigned him a servant to set him on his way,
To fare with him over the fells to frustrate delay,
So that he could go through the groves and glades by a good
            Quick road.
        Gawain then gave the host
        The honour and thanks he owed,
        But on the lovely ladies most
        His dear adieux bestowed.

XXXIV

So he spoke to them sadly, sorrowing as he kissed,
And urged on them heartily his endless thanks,
And they in turn their compliments thrust on him,

Commending him to Christ with cries of chill sadness.
Then from the whole household he honourably took his leave,
Making all the men that he met amends
For their several services and solicitous care,
For they had been busily attendant, bustling about him;
And all he saw were as sad to say farewell
As if they had dwelt with the worthy man always.
Then the lords led him with lights to his chamber,
And blithely brought him to bed to rest.
If he slept – I dare not assert it – less soundly than usual,
There was much on his mind for the morrow, if he meant to give
   It thought.
  Let him lie there still,
  He almost has what he sought;
  So tarry a while until
  The process I report.

PART FOUR

I

Now the New Year neared, the night passed,
Daylight drove off the darkness as the Deity bids.
But wild was the weather the world awoke to;
Bitterly the clouds cast down cold on the earth,
Inflicting on the flesh flails from the north.
Bleakly the snow blustered, and beasts were frozen;
The whistling wind wailed from the heights,
Driving great drifts deep in the dales.
Keenly the lord listened as he lay in his bed;
Though his lids were closed, he was sleeping little.
Every cock that crew recalled to him his tryst.
Before the day had dawned, he had dressed himself,
For the light from a lamp illuminated his chamber.
He summoned his servant, who swiftly answered,
Commanded that his mail-coat and mount's saddle be brought.
The man fared forth and fetched him his armour,
And set Sir Gawain's array in splendid style.
First he clad him in his clothes to counter the cold,
Then in his other armour which had been well kept;
His breast- and belly-armour had been burnished bright,
And the rusty rings of his rich mail-coat rolled clean;[1]
And all being as fresh as at first, he was fain to give thanks
       Indeed.

1. One method of ridding armour of rust and dirt was to put it into a barrel of sand and roll it about.

Each wiped and polished piece
He donned with due heed.
The gayest from here to Greece,
The strong man sent for his steed.

II

WHILE he was putting on apparel of the most princely kind
His surcoat, with the crest clearly worked
Environed on velvet with valuable gems,
Embellished and bound with embroidered seam-strips,
And finely trimmed with fairest furs on the inside –
He did not leave the lace belt, the lady's gift:
For his own good, Gawain did not forget that!
When he had strapped the sword on his smooth hips,
The knight lapped his loins with his love-token twice,
Quickly wrapped it with relish round himself.
The green silken girdle suited the gallant well,
Backed by the royal red cloth that richly showed.
But he wore the girdle in his gear not for its great worth,
Nor through pride in the pendants, in spite of their polish,
Nor the gleaming gold which glinted on the ends,
But to save himself when of necessity he must
Stand an evil stroke, not resisting it with knife
        Or sword.
    When ready and robed aright,
    Out came the comely lord;
    To the men of name and might
    His thanks in plenty poured.

III

THEN was Gringolet got ready, that great huge horse.
Having been assiduously stabled in seemly quarters,
The fiery steed was fit and fretting for a gallop.
Sir Gawain stepped to him and, inspecting his coat,
Said earnestly to himself, asserting with truth,
'Here in this castle is a company whose conduct is honourable.
The man who maintains them, may he have joy!
The delightful lady, may love befall her!
Thus for charity they cherish a chance guest
Honourably and open-handedly; may He on high,
The King of Heaven, requite them and their company too.
And if I could live any longer in lands on earth,
Some rich recompense, if I could, I should readily give you.'
Then he stepped into the stirrup and swung aloft.
His man[1] showed him his shield; on his shoulder he put it,
Gave the spur to Gringolet with his gold-spiked heels,
And started off, not staying on the stone pavement
        To prance.
    His man was mounted, fit,
    Laden with spear and lance.
    'This castle to Christ I commit:
    May He its fortune enhance!'

IV

THE drawbridge was let down and the broad double gates
Were unbarred and borne open on both sides.

1. This man is of course not Sir Gawain's squire, as he rode forth from
Camelot alone, but the guide supplied by Sir Bertilak.

Passing over the planks, the prince blessed himself
And praised the kneeling porter, who proffered him 'Good day',
And prayed God to grant that Gawain would be saved.
And Gawain went on his way with the one man
To put him on the right path for that perilous place
Where the sad assault must be received by him.
By bluffs where boughs were bare they passed,
Climbed by cliffs where the cold clung:
Under the high clouds, ugly mists
Merged damply with the moors and melted on the mountains;
Each hill had a hat, a huge mantle of mist.
On the heights about them brooks burst forth boiling,
Showering down sharply in shimmering cascades.
Their way through the woods was wonderfully wild;
Till it was soon time for the sun to ascend on high
    That day.
   They were on a lofty hill
   Where snow beside them lay,
   When the servant[1] stopped still
   And told his master to stay.

V

'FOR I have guided you to this ground, Sir Gawain, at this time
And now you are not far from the noted place

1. More than one commentator has suggested that this servant is the Green
Knight in yet another shape. In the analogues the Tempter or Antagonist often
assumed an unexpected guise in order to subject the hero to an extra ordeal.
Since the Antagonist (Sir Bertilak or the Green Knight) is never shown to us
at the same time as the servant guide, and this functionary has a directness of
speech like that of the Green Knight, the suggestion seems to be a good one.

Which you have searched for and sought with such special zeal.
But I must say to you, forsooth, since I know you,
And you are a lord whom I love with no little regard,
Take my governance as guide, and it shall go better for you.
For the place is perilous that you are pressing towards.
In that wilderness dwells the worst man in the world,
For he is valiant and fierce and fond of fighting,
And mightier than any man that may be on earth,
And his body is bigger than the best four
In Arthur's house, or Hector, or any other.
At the Green Chapel he gains his great adventures.
No man passes that place, however proud in arms,
Without being dealt a death-blow by his dreadful hand.
For he is an immoderate man, to mercy a stranger;
For whether churl or chaplain by the chapel rides,
Monk or mass-priest or man of other kind,
He thinks it as convenient to kill him as keep alive himself.
Therefore I say, as certainly as you sit in your saddle,
If you go there, you will get your doom, if the gallant man wishes,
Take my troth for it, though you had twenty lives
            And more.
      He has lived here since long ago
      And filled the field with gore.
      You cannot counter his blow,
      It strikes so sudden and sore.

                              VI

'THEREFORE, good Sir Gawain, leave the grim man alone!
Ride by another route, to some region remote.

Go, for God's sake, and may He grace your fortune!
And I shall go home again and undertake
To swear solemnly by God and his saints as well
(By my halidom, so help me God, and every other oath)
To keep silent concerning you, not saying to a soul
What I fully know, that you fled from the fellow.'
'Great thanks,' replied Gawain, somewhat galled, and said,
'It is worthy of you to wish for my well-being, man,
And I believe you would loyally lock it in your heart.
But however quiet you kept it, if I quit this place,
Fled from the fellow in the fashion you propose,
I should become a cowardly knight with no excuse whatever.
But I will go to the Green Chapel, to get what Fate sends,
Have whatever words I wish with that worthy,
Weal or woe betide: and that is what Fate decides
      Alone:
    Though he is grim with his axe[1]
    And not easily overthrown,
    Our Lord is wise and lacks
    No strength to save his own.'

VII

'By Mary!' said the other man. 'If you mean what you say,
You are determined to take all your trouble on yourself.

1. The word in the original is 'stave'. Editors seem to disagree about the meaning, but an interesting suggestion by Tolkien and Gordon is 'club'. They say that a club is the sort of weapon one would expect to find used by the haunter of a fairy mound, and quote from the Mabinogion an example of a black man on a mound who wields one. Both editors justify their conclusions on linguistic grounds. Since our poem is dominated by the mental picture of a huge axe-wielder, I have followed Gollancz.

If you wish to lose your life, I'll no longer hinder you.
Here's your lance for your hand, your helmet for your head.
Ride down this rough track round yonder cliff
Till you arrive in a rugged ravine at the bottom,
Then look about on the flat, on your left hand,
And you will view there in the vale that very chapel,
And the grim gallant who guards it always.
Now, noble Gawain, good-bye in God's name.
For all the gold on God's earth I would not go with you,
Nor foot it an inch further through this forest as your fellow.'
Whereupon he wrenched at his reins, that rider in the woods,
Hit the horse with his heels as hard as he could,
Sent him leaping along, and left the knight there
           Alone.
      'By God!' said Gawain, 'I swear
      I will not weep or groan:
      Being given to God's good care,
      My trust in Him shall be shown.'

                         VIII

THEN he gave the spur to Gringolet and galloped down the path,
Thrust through a thicket there by a bank,
And rode down the rough slope right into the ravine.[1]

1. Various locations have been suggested for the eerie setting of Gawain's last
trial. The Peak District and the Staffordshire moorlands have been mooted,
as these are the nearest high regions to the Wirral, the last place mentioned in
Sir Gawain's itinerary. According to Mr R. W. V. Elliott, the author of an
article in *The Times* of 21st May 1958, there is some evidence in the poem to
suggest that the poet had in mind the region of Swythamley Park in Staffordshire, where the scenery is like that described in the poem, complete with
legend-haunted natural chapel.

Then he searched about, but it seemed savage and wild,
And no sign did he see of any sort of dwelling;
But on both sides banks, beetling and steep,
And great crooked crags, cruelly jagged;
The bristling barbs of rock seemed to brush the sky.
Then he held in his horse, halted there,
Scanned on every side in search of the chapel.
He saw no such thing anywhere, which seemed remarkable,
Save, not far off, on the flat, a fairy mound apparently,
A smooth-surfaced barrow by the side of a stream
Which flowed forth there in a fall of water,
Foaming and frothing as if feverishly boiling.
The knight, urging his horse, pressed onwards to the mound,
Stepped determinedly from the stirrup, attached to a tree
The reins, hooking them round a rough branch,
And went to the barrow, which he walked round, inspecting,
Wondering what in the world it might be.
It had a hole in each end and on either side,
And was overgrown with grass in great patches.
All hollow it was within, only an old cavern
Or the crevice of an ancient crag: he could not explain it
          Aright.
    'O God, is the Chapel Green
    This mound?' said the noble knight.
    'At such might Satan be seen
    Saying matins at midnight.'

IX

'Now certainly the place is deserted,' said Gawain,
'It is a hideous oratory, all overgrown,
And well graced for the gallant garbed in green
To deal out his devotions in the Devil's fashion.
Now I feel in my five wits, it is the Fiend himself
That has tricked me into this tryst, to destroy me here.
This is a chapel of mischance – checkmate to it!
It is the most evil holy place I ever entered.'
With his high helmet on his head, and holding his lance,
He roamed up to the roof of that rough dwelling.
Then from that height he heard, from a hard rock
On the bank beyond the brook, a barbarous noise.
What! It clattered amid the cliffs fit to cleave them apart,
As if a great scythe were being ground on a grindstone there.
What! It whirred and it whetted, like water in a mill.
What! It made a rushing, ringing din, rueful to hear.[1]
'By God!' then said Gawain, 'that is going on,
I suppose, as a salute to myself, to greet me
> Hard by.
> God's will be warranted:
> "Alas!" is a craven cry.
> No din shall make me dread
> Although today I die.'

---

1. Only one of the parallel romances mentions the whetting, and then only briefly. This making of splendid dramatic moments is characteristic of the *Sir Gawain* poet at his best.

X

THEN the courteous knight called out clamorously,
'Who holds sway here and has an assignation with me?
For the good knight Gawain is on the ground here.
If anyone there wants anything, wend your way hither fast,
And further your needs either now, or not at all.'
'Bide there!' said one on the bank above his head,
'And you shall swiftly receive what I once swore to give you.'
Yet he pressed on apace for a period with the din,
Turning away to go on whetting, before he would descend.
Then he thrust himself round a thick crag through a hole,
Whirling round a wedge of rock with a frightful weapon,
A Danish axe[1] duly honed for dealing the blow,
With a broad biting edge, bow-bent by the haft,
Ground on a grindstone, and by the gleaming lace
It measured fully four feet in breadth.
And the gallant in green was garbed as at first,
His looks and limbs the same, his locks and beard;
Save that steadily on his feet he strode on the ground,
Setting the handle to the stony earth and stalking beside it.
He would not wade through the water when he came to it,
But vaulted over on his axe, then with huge strides
Advanced violently and fiercely along the bank
        On the snow.
    Sir Gawain went to greet
    The knight, not bowing low.

1. This Danish axe, so called because the Vikings used it, was, according to the
O.E.D., 'a kind of battle-axe with a very long blade, and usually without a
spike on the back'. The weapon the Green Knight bore at King Arthur's court
was a guisarm, or battle-axe complete with spike.

The man said, 'Sir so sweet,
   You keep your trysts, I trow.'

XI

'GAWAIN,' said the green knight, 'may God guard you!
You are welcome to my dwelling, I warrant you,
And you have travelled here on time as a true man ought,
And you are cognisant of the compact accorded between us.
This time a twelvemonth ago you took your portion,
And now at this New Year I should nimbly requite you.
And we are on our own here in this valley,
Without people to part us, play as we will.
Take your helmet off your head, and have your payment here.
And offer no more argument or action than I did
When you whipped off my head with one stroke.'
'No,' said Gawain, 'by God who gave me a soul,
The grievous gash to come I grudge you not at all;
Strike but the one stroke and I shall stand still
And offer you no hindrance: you may act freely,
      I swear.'
   Head bent, Sir Gawain bowed,
   And showed the bright flesh bare.
   He behaved as if uncowed,
   Being loth to display his care.

XII

THEN the gallant in green quickly got ready,
Heaved his horrid weapon on high to hit Gawain,

With all the brute force in his body bearing it aloft,
Swinging savagely enough to strike him dead.
Had it driven down as direly as he aimed,
The daring dauntless man would have died with the blow.
But Gawain glanced up at the grim axe beside him
As it came shooting through the shivering air to shatter him,
And his shoulders shrank slightly from the sharp edge.
The other suddenly stayed the descending axe,
And then reproved the prince with many proud words:
'You are not Gawain,' said the gallant, 'whose goodness is such
That by hill or hollow no army ever frightened him;
For now you flinch for fear before you feel harm.
I could not contemplate such cowardice from him.
I neither flinched nor fled when you let fly your blow,
Nor offered any quibble in the house of King Arthur.
My head flew to my feet, but flee I did not.
Yet you quail cravenly though unscathed so far.
So it behoves me to be called the better man
            Therefore.'
        Said Gawain, 'Not again
        Shall I flinch as I did before,
        But if my head pitch to the plain,
        It's off for evermore.

XIII

'But be brisk, man, by your faith, and bring me to the poin ;
Deal me my destiny and do it out of hand,
For I shall stand your stroke, not starting at all
Till your axe has hit me. Here is my oath on it.'

'Have at you then,' said the other, heaving up his axe,
Behaving as angrily as if he were mad.
He menaced him mightily, but gave the man no hit,
Smartly withholding his hand without hurting him.
Gawain waited unswerving, with not a wavering limb,
But stood still as a stone or the stump of a tree
Gripping the rocky ground with a hundred grappling roots.
Then again the green knight began to gird:
'So now you have a whole heart I must hit you.
May the high knighthood which Arthur conferred
Preserve you and save your neck, if so it avail you!'
Then said Gawain, storming with sudden rage,
'Thrash on, you thrustful fellow, you threaten too much.
I deem you are in dread of your own doughty self.'
'Forsooth,' said the other, 'you speak so fiercely
I will no longer lengthen matters by delaying your business,
      I vow.'
    He stood astride to smite,
    Lips pouting, puckered brow.
    Gawain grieved at his plight,
    For nothing could save him now.

XIV

UP went the axe at once and hurtled down straight
At the naked neck with its knife-like edge.
Though it swung down savagely, slight was the wound,
A mere snick on the side, so that the skin was broken.
Through the fair fat to the flesh fell the blade,
And over his shoulders the shimmering blood shot to the ground.

When Sir Gawain saw his gore glinting on the snow,
He sprang a spear's-length away, spread-eagling his feet,
Hurriedly heaved his helmet on to his head,
And shrugging his shoulders, shot his shield to the front,
Swung out his bright sword and said fiercely
(For never had the knight since being nursed by his mother
Been so buoyantly happy, so blithe in this world),
'Cease your blows, sir, strike me no more.
I have sustained a stroke here unresistingly,
And if you offer any more I shall earnestly reply,
Resisting, rest assured, with the most rancorous
          Despite.
     The single stroke is wrought
     To which we pledged our plight
     In high King Arthur's court:
     Enough now, therefore, knight!'

XV

THE bold man stood back and bent over his axe,
Putting the haft to earth, and leaning on the head.
He gazed at Sir Gawain on the ground before him,
Considering the spirited and stout way he stood,
Audacious in arms; his heart warmed to him.
Then he gave utterance gladly in his great voice,
With resounding speech saying to the knight,
'Bold man, do not be so bloodily resolute.
No one here has offered you evil discourteously,
Contrary to the covenant made at King Arthur's court.
I promised a stroke, which you received: consider yourself paid.

I cancel all other obligations of whatever kind.
If I had been more active, perhaps I could
Have made you suffer by striking a savager stroke.
First in foolery I made a feint at striking,
Not rending you with a riving cut — and right I was,
On account of the first night's covenant we accorded;
For you truthfully kept your trust in troth with me,
Giving me your gains, as a good man should.
The further feinted blow was for the following day,
When you kissed my comely wife, and the kisses came to me:
For those two things, harmlessly I thrust twice at you
          Feinted blows.
     Truth for truth's the word;
     No need for dread, God knows.
     From your failure at the third
     The tap you took arose.

XVI

'FOR that braided belt you wear belongs to me.
I am well aware that my own wife gave it you.
Your conduct and your kissings are completely known to me,
And the wooing of my wife — my work set it on.
I sent her to essay you, and you certainly seem
To be the most perfect paladin ever to pace the earth.
As the pearl to the white pea in precious worth,
So in good faith is Gawain to other gay knights.
But here your faith failed you, you flagged somewhat, sir,
Yet it was not for a well-wrought thing, nor for wooing either,
But for love of your life, which is less blameworthy.'

The other strong man stood in suspense a while,
So filled with fury that his flesh trembled,
And the blood from his breast burst forth in his face.
He shrank for shame at what the chevalier spoke of.
The first words the fair knight could frame were:
'Curses on both cowardice and covetousness!
Their vice and villainy is virtue's destroyer.'
Then he took the knot, with a twist twitched it loose,
And in great anger gave the girdle to the knight.
'Lo! There is the false thing, foul fortune befall it!
I being craven about our encounter, cowardice
Connived with covetousness to corrupt my nature
And the liberality and loyalty belonging to chivalry.
Now I am faulty and false and found fearful always.
In the train of treachery and untruth go misery
        And woe;
    I acknowledge, knight, how ill
    My shameful faults here show.
    May I gain your good will
    And henceforth heedful go!'

                        XVII

THEN the other lord laughed and politely said,
'In my view you have made amends for your misdemeanour;
You have acknowledged your faults fully in fair confession,
And plainly done penance at the point of my axe.
You are absolved of your sin and as stainless now
As if you had never fallen in fault since first you were born.
As for the gold-hemmed girdle, I give it you, sir.

Seeing it is as green as my gown, Sir Gawain, you may
Think about this trial when you throng in company
With paragons of princes, for it is a perfect token,
At knightly gatherings, of the great adventure at the Green Chapel.
You shall come back to my castle this cold New Year
To revel for the rest of this rich feast, leading
   A gay life.'
  Then with a laugh the lord
  Said, 'You and my winsome wife
  Shall come to sweet accord
  After your strenuous strife.'

XVIII

'No, forsooth,' said the knight, seizing his helmet,
And doffing it with dignity as he delivered his thanks,
'My stay has sufficed me. Still, luck go with you!
May He who bestows all good, honour you with it!
And commend me to the courteous lady, your comely wife;
Indeed, my due regards to both dear ladies,
Who with their wanton wiles have thus waylaid their knight.
But it is no marvel for a foolish man to be maddened thus
And saddled with sorrow by the sleights of women.
For here on earth was Adam taken in by one,
And Solomon by many such, and Samson likewise;
Delilah dealt him his doom; and David, later still,
Was blinded by Bathsheba, and badly suffered for it.[1]

1. This sort of inveighing against womankind in general was a homiletic
commonplace of the Middle Ages, when woman's social status was low
although, paradoxically, the common form of religious expression was
Mariolatrous.

These four having been fretted by their falsehoods, it would be fair joy
To love them but not believe them, if a lord could,
For these four were the finest whom Fortune favoured
Of all under the Kingdom of Heaven who ever
    Loved well;
  And all were at last brought low
  By a lover's malignant spell;
  So grant me forgiveness, though
  To women's wiles I fell.

XIX

'BUT your girdle,' said Gawain, 'God requite you for it!
Not for the glorious gold shall I gladly wear it,
Nor for the stuff nor the silk nor the side pendants,
Nor for its worth, fine workmanship or wonderful honour;
But as a sign of my sin I shall see it often,
Remembering with remorse, when I am mounted in glory,
The fault and faintheartedness of the perverse flesh,
How vulnerable it is to vile advice and sin.
So when pride shall prick me for my prowess in arms,
One look at this love-lace shall make me lowly again.
But one demand I make of you, may it not incommode you:
Since you are master of the demesne I have remained in a while,
Make known, by your knighthood, – and now may He above,
Sitting on high and holding up heaven, requite you! –
How you pronounce your true name; and no more requests.'
'Truly,' the other told him, 'I shall tell you my title.

Bertilak of the High Desert[1] I am called here in this land.
I was entirely transformed and made terrible of hue
Through the might of Morgan the Fay,[2] who remains in my house.
Through the wiles of her witchcraft, a lore well learned,
Many of the magical arts of Merlin[3] has she acquired,
For once she lavished her love delightfully
On that susceptible sage, a sorcerer your knights know
       By name.
    So "Morgan the goddess"
    She accordingly became;
    The proudest she can oppress
    And to her purpose tame.

XX

'SHE sent me forth in this form to your famous hall
To put to the proof the great pride of the house,
The reputation for high renown of the Round Table.
To rob you of your wits she bewitched me in this weird way,
And to grieve Guinevere and goad her to death
With ghastly fear of that ghost's ghoulish speaking
With his head in his hand before the high table.
That is the aged beldame who is at home:
She is indeed your own aunt, Arthur's half-sister,

---

1. Bertilak de Hautdesert. The name Bertilak or Bercilak is Celtic. 'Haut-desert' may refer either to the Peak District, or possibly to the waste place among the hills where the Green Chapel is. Professor Tolkien points out that 'desert' went into Celtic languages from Latin, and was used to describe the place where a hermit lived.

2. Morgan the Fay. See Appendix Seven.

3. Merlin. See Appendix Eight.

Daughter of the Duchess of Tintagel[1] who in due course,
By Uther, was mother of Arthur, who now holds sway.
Therefore I beg you, bold sir, come back to your aunt,
Make merry in my house, for my men love you,
And by my faith, fair sir, I fancy you as well
As any gallant under God, for your great honesty.'
But Gawain firmly refused with a final negative.
They clasped and kissed, commending each other
To the Prince of Paradise, and parted on the cold ground
       Right there.
    Gawain on steed serene
    Spurred to court with courage fair,
    And the gallant garbed in green
    To wherever he would elsewhere.

XXI

Now Gawain goes riding on Gringolet
In lonely lands, his life saved by grace.
Often he stayed at a house, and often in the open,
And was victor in various adventures in the vales,
Which at this time I do not intend to tell you about.
The hurt he had had in his neck was healed,
And the glittering girdle that girt him round
Obliquely, like a baldric, was bound by his side
And laced under the left arm with a lasting knot,

1. This Duchess of Tintagel was Igerne or Igraine, the wife of Gorlois of
Cornwall. Uther Pendragon assumed the likeness of Gorlois through the magic
of Merlin, and so won his way into the castle to beget Arthur. (As in *King Lear*
and elsewhere, it is bastardy that produces the vigorous strain.) On the death
of Gorlois, Uther married Igerne.

In token that he was taken in a tarnishing sin;
And so he came to court, quite unscathed.
When the great ones knew of good Gawain's arrival,
There was general jubilation at the joyful news.
The King kissed the knight, and the Queen likewise,
And so did many a staunch noble who sought to salute him.
They all asked him about his expedition,
And he truthfully told them of his tribulations –
What chanced at the chapel, the good cheer of the knight,
The love of the lady, and lastly, the girdle.
He displayed the scar of the snick on his neck
Where the bold man's blow had hit, his bad faith to
          Proclaim;
     He groaned at his disgrace,
     Unfolding his ill-fame,
     And blood suffused his face
     When he showed his mark of shame.

XXII

'Look, this is the lace, my lord,' said the knight,
'This band on my neck bears witness to my blameworthiness,
This is my bane and debasement, the burden I bear
For being caught by cowardice and covetousness.
This is the figure of the faithlessness that was found in me,
Which I must needs wear while I live.
For sin cannot be concealed without sorry luck succeeding,
Since, when it is once fixed, it will never be worked loose.'
The King and all the court comforted the knight,
And all the lords and ladies belonging to the Table

Laughed at it loudly, and concluded amiably
That each brave man of the brotherhood should bear a baldric,[1]
A band, obliquely about him, of a bright green,
Of the same hue as Sir Gawain's, and for his sake wear it.
So it ranked as renown to the Round Table,
And an everlasting honour to him who had it,
As is rendered in Romance's rarest book.
Thus in the days of Arthur this exploit was achieved,
To which the books of Brutus[2] bear witness;
After the bold baron, Brutus, came here,
The siege and the assault being ceased at Troy
          Before.
      News of such high renown
      Was heard here often of yore.
      Now Christ with His thorny crown
      Grant us His grace evermore! AMEN.

HONY SOYT QUI MAL
PENCE

1. The conjunction of the green baldric and the motto of the Order of the Garter has been taken to mean that the poem was written for the institution of the Garter; but that order was founded by Edward III in about 1347, and its distinctive badge was a garter of dark blue velvet. The ballad of the Green Knight, however, deliberately associates the Order of the Bath with this story. Ritual purification of knights by bathing appears to have been practised in England as long ago as the eleventh century, and the Order was formally constituted for the coronation of Henry IV in 1399. But no insignia were worn by the holders. When revived four hundred years later, the Order of the Bath had a crimson ribbon; no trace of green is found anywhere, although Froissart, as quoted by Selden (1672), refers to a silk ribbon.

2. Any chronicle of British times might be called a 'Brutus book'.

THE MANUSCRIPT

Sir Gawain and the Green Knight exists in a single vellum manuscript in the Cotton Collection in the British Museum – MS Nero A.x. On this small manuscript, which measures only about seven inches by five, *Sir Gawain* is the last of four poems, the other three being *Pearl*, *Cleanliness*, and *Patience*. There is strong linguistic, stylistic, and metrical evidence of their all being by the same poet, but his name is not known for certain.

The writing, which is in the same hand throughout, is late four-teenth-century, and not only has the ink become faded, but some of the pages were closed before the ink was dry: hence the great difficulty of reading the poem, although many of the blurred letters have been interpreted by reading the blotted impression with a mirror. The two standard editions, however, generally provide a fair way for the reader. The language is agreed to be North Midland or, more especially, the dialect of Cheshire and South Lancashire.

The manuscript is illustrated by twelve pictures, four of which represent scenes from *Sir Gawain*. Only one of these, which shows Sir Gawain lying in bed and the Lady touching the end of his beard with the middle finger of her left hand, is at all clear. But since the details of the picture do not correspond precisely with any situation described in the poem, and the artist is of inferior merit, it may be doubted whether the illustrations are strictly contemporary, although some scholars think they are.

THEORIES ABOUT THE POET

THERE is a fascination in probing anonymity, especially remote anonymity, which may sometimes lead to excess. If the quest for an author's identity becomes an obsession, his name and life come to seem more important than his work. Yet, although most of us may be content with the revealed life of the work, there will always be people rightly dedicated to the prospect of disinterring the true identity of a lost major artist.

So it is with the poet of *Sir Gawain and the Green Knight*, for whom several names have been suggested and discarded. One idea, put forward by O. Cargill and Miss Schlauch, taking as departure point the similarity in style between *Pearl* and *Sir Gawain*, is that the infant girl lamented in the former poem was Margaret, daughter of the Earl of Pembroke and granddaughter of Edward III, and that the poet is accordingly one of Pembroke's clerks, perhaps John Donne or John Prat. A much earlier suggestion, based on the writing at the beginning of *Sir Gawain*, in a fifteenth-century hand, of 'Hugo de', was that the poet was the Scottish author of alliterative romances, Huchown: but the style of other surviving works attributed to Huchown does not correspond with that of *Sir Gawain*. Sir Israel Gollancz proposed Ralph Strode, the Oxford scholastic philosopher and logician, and C. O. Chapman proposed John of Erghome, author of *The Prophecy of John of Bridlington*, but neither of these suggestions has been generally accepted.

The most interesting, and to me convincing, suggestion is that made by Mr Ormerod Greenwood in the introduction to his verse translation published by the Lion and Unicorn Press in 1956. The full evidence, with its basis of Numerology (which had high standing among mystics and philosophers of former ages), textual puns, and provenance, is too long to be given in full, and the curious are referred to Mr Greenwood's work. Hugh Mascy, or Hugo de Masci, is the conjectured name. The Masseys are an old Cheshire family ('as many Massies as asses' is a local proverb quoted by Mr Greenwood), with which is found associated, a century later, the manuscript of *St Erkenwald*, a fifth poem often ascribed to the *Sir Gawain* poet. The geography of *Sir Gawain* firmly links it with the Massey district, and the names Hugo and Margery (the latter being the name of the child mourned in *Pearl*) abound in the Massey family in the fourteenth century.

The numerological evidence of authorship is found chiefly in *Pearl*, which, like *Sir Gawain*, has a hundred and one stanzas. The numerical value, in the medieval alphabet, of the letters in the name Hugo de Masci, is 101, and the seal inscriptions of the family, ending with the name Masci, end CI, or 101. The arrangement of *Pearl*, which begins with twelve groups of five stanzas each of twelve lines, and its total number of lines, 1212, takes on additional meaning when considered with the fact that the name Margery Masci has twelve letters, and that there are significantly placed puns on the word 'Masci' in the poem. Mr Greenwood thus finds the family name 'Masci', the name of the daughter 'Margery', and the name of the poet 'Hugo de' hammered home in a series of puns and numerical values throughout the extraordinarily complicated structure of the poem. This structure seems to me only to make sense from the point of view of the poet and his public if some key, such as that suggested by Mr Greenwood, will unlock its secret. But, as Mr Greenwood writes, his attribution must remain short of proof 'until a Hugh can be found with a daughter Margery who died in infancy'.

APPENDIX THREE

SIR GAWAIN

No character in the whole of Arthurian romance undergoes such metamorphosis as Gawain. Beginning, apparently, as an Irish hero, he passes into the Arthurian cycle as the pattern of bravery and courtesy. He holds first place at Arthur's court, but in later Romances he is superseded by other heroes, like Lancelot, and ends as a treacherous and almost effeminate creature in Malory.

The presumed source of the Beheading Game part of the 'Sir Gawain' story has as its hero Cuchulain, some of whose characteristics, particularly those which show him as a sun-hero, are possessed by Gawain in different romances. Gawain's father, King Lot of the Orkneys, has been traced through Welsh Lloch to the Irish god Lug, Cuchulain's father, who was the colour of the setting sun – red – from sunset to sunrise. In the early stories Gawain's strength, like Cuchulain's, increases until midday and then declines towards evening, and he inherits from the Irish hero his diadem and golden hair. Moreover, it is Gawain, and not Arthur, who is the owner of the light-giving sword Excalibur. In Welsh legend, before the full impact of the Arthurian cycle was felt, there is a Gwri Gwalltenryn 'of the golden hair', who passes on this characteristic to Gwalchmai, the Welsh Gawain. Possibly Gwalchmai was hero of a pre-Arthurian cycle of adventures, and so became easily identifiable with the new hero. But Mr Robert Graves, in 'The White Goddess', notes that Gwalchmai ('hawk of may'), Gwalchaved ('hawk of summer'), and Gwalch gwyn ('white hawk') are mystical names, and that the Welsh court-bards always likened their royal patrons to hawks: he says the last two names are respectively early forms of Galahad and Gawain. The hawk is of course a sun-bird.

In the Grail romances, and as Gwalchmai in the Welsh Triads, Gawain is persistently represented as a healer well versed in herbal remedies. Miss Jessie Weston, in her *From Ritual to Romance*, sees Gawain as the medicine man who, in the fertility ritual underlying the mystery of the Grail (the Church was opposed to the Grail stories), restores to life the Spirit of Vegetation. Brought up on Malory, we may forget that Gawain was the original Grail hero, and that the story on which Chrétien de Troyes and others based their Grail romances was a non-Christian Grail poem by the Welshman Bleheris.

One other primitive solar characteristic of Gawain's, which we find in our poem, is his eternal youth. This he received as a gift when he visited the fairy island inhabited only by women, which in Irish tradition sometimes represents the other world.

Although the name *Gawain* and all the pre-Romance characteristics of the hero derive from Celtic tradition, it is as the model of chivalry, and especially as the perfect upholder of courtesy, that Gawain earned his medieval fame, and it is this conception of him which our poet further exalts. Among Sir Gawain's virtues is his concern for the vanquished: to the brusque and heartless Sir Kay, Sir Gawain is the perfect foil, in whom the old epic boasting before and after battle is transformed into Christian humility. Gawain retains, even in his degeneration, his good reputation in matters affecting women, which of course receives fine expression in our poem. He never has an illicit affair, as Tristan and Lancelot do. In one romance, in order to save King Arthur's life, he weds and treats chivalrously the foul hag Ragnell, who not unexpectedly turns into a beautiful girl.

It is particularly in the English Arthurian poems and stories that Gawain achieves his perfection, and almost becomes a national hero. William of Malmesbury (d. 1143) records the existence of his tomb in Wales, and all the English romancers, from Geoffrey of Monmouth to our poet, unhesitatingly put him first among King Arthur's knights. 'Gavin' is still a popular name in the north of England.

KING ARTHUR

KING Arthur is too well known to need a miniature monograph here. He appears to have a double origin, and both sources are well attested in ancient Welsh writings. The best-known tradition makes him a Welsh or British chieftain of the fifth or sixth century. A tradition which is probably earlier, though it has survived in manuscripts of later date, makes him a kind of King of Fairyland, belonging to the same group of Celtic mythological characters as Gawain's predecessor, Gwalchmai. Hence arises the double process which he underwent in the medieval mind. By that of the Romance writers and historians, he is elevated, and made head of the court of chivalry, as in our poem. He is the perfect patron, springing with semi-divine youthfulness, but human too, and passionate in his service to the only sanctioned decorum. Popular tradition, on the other hand, building on the pseudo-history and naturally adding to the Christian Arthurian romances its own folk notions, stresses the magical aspect, and especially his immortality. As a national hero who would one day return, he was supposed to be still living under the ground with his knights, an idea which occasionally brought him into association with the Prince of Darkness. But we have been warned recently against making a convenient distinction between the literary and the folk traditions of the Middle Ages; and it is therefore not surprising to find a scholar, Alanus de Insulis, writing in about 1175 that anyone who said Arthur was dead could not escape stoning.

Although it was a ninth-century Welshman, Nennius, who introduced Arthur as a national hero and thaumaturge, it is as a wider, British, hero that he established himself. Thus it was to Arthur that Milton's first musings on his projected national epic led him.

CAMELOT

It is disappointing to record that the location of 'Camelot' is as uncertain as ever, and that nothing more positive than intelligent surmise can be applied to the indications. These seem to be only mythological or literary: hence, the *Encyclopaedia Britannica* and the *Standard Dictionary of Folklore, Mythology and Legend,* in remarkably similar entries, offer us Caerleon-upon-Usk in Monmouthshire, Camelford in Cornwall, Queen's Camel in Somerset, and, following Malory, Winchester. There remain the local traditions which, in a country like Britain, through which so many races and cultures swept in the first millennium, would be likely to confuse the remains and legends of one set of invaders with those of another.

Caerleon (Castra Legionis of the Romans) seems to be mentioned in connexion with Camelot merely because there was an old fortress there. Roman occupation might leave behind legends of a distant race, which Geoffrey of Monmouth would pick up. He wrote that Arthur was crowned at Caerleon – and his word has been sufficient for all ages until real history began to be written. But Geoffrey was a Monmouth man. The Roman amphitheatre at Caerleon, one of the few in Britain to have been fully excavated, is known locally as 'King Arthur's Round Table'.

Camelford has the advantage of being near Tintagel and Boscastle, sites of famous events in Arthurian romance, but seems scarcely central enough for a king to have used it as a capital from which to rule the southwest of England. Leland, the sixteenth-century antiquary, followed by Selden a century later, places the battle of the Camlan here, partly, no doubt, because there is a 'King Arthur's Grave' at Camelford. Tennyson's Camelot is here too.

Malory's suggestion of Winchester may derive from his knowledge that Winchester was the seat of the Saxon kings.

South Cadbury, the hill fortress in Somerset which boasts an accumulation of Arthurian place-names and legends, and is near two rivers with names bearing the right beginning of 'Cam-', seems a more likely Camelot, although there is no direct evidence. Ed. J. Burrow in his *Ancient Earthworks and Camps of Somerset* (1924), remarks that it is the largest and most formidable of the late Celtic fortresses in the West Country, having a raised area of eighteen acres above a quadruple rampart and ditch nearly 150 feet above the valley floor. The three trenches separating the ramparts average twelve yards in depth and were cut out of the solid rock, while the ramparts average thirty-five feet in height. At one end of the plateau on top is a raised platform called 'Arthur's Castle' or 'Arthur's Palace'. There are two wells within the fortress area, at one of which King Arthur and his men are supposed to water their horses after their ride round the hill at full moon. One legend gives their horses silver shoes; another tips their swords with fire, which helps Mr K. E. Maltwood, in his *Guide to Glastonbury's 'Temple of the Stars'* (1950), to suggest that we may have some evidence of the worship of a shadowy sky-god, Camulos, whose attribute was creative light. Local tradition has it that Cadbury Castle is hollow, and the subterranean residence of the Knights of the Round Table.

There is no clue, in *Sir Gawain and the Green Knight*, to the location of Camelot. But if Sir Gawain's route from Camelot to the Wirral is to be as wild as the poet makes it, Arthur's seat should be in the West Country or South Wales, and not southern England.

APPENDIX SIX

THE PENTANGLE

THE Pentangle, or five-pointed star, which may be drawn without taking the pencil from the paper (hence 'The Endless Knot'), is assigned to Sir Gawain only in this poem. Elsewhere in Romance, his shield bears one of the usual heraldic creatures – a lion, gryphon, or eagle – in gold upon green. But of course any knight could have one of these as his device, without any special significance attaching thereto. It is characteristic of our poet's learned and idealistic approach to assign to Gawain the mysterious Pentangle. Of the two general forms of the device, the elongated and the regular, the former appears to be best fitted for working on a shield.

The Pentangle, the most important sign in magic, the *quint*essence of the alchemists, is about as old as history. It is first found scratched on Babylonian pottery from Ur, and from that time onward figures prominently in oriental and near eastern religions as a mystic symbol of perfection. The Pythagoreans used it, probably because five is the perfect number, being the marriage of the first masculine number, three, with the first feminine number, two (unity not being a true number). In one of the Gnostic systems it was the passport to the Kingdom of Light: the Virgin Sophia would admit to her realm only bearers of the seal of the Pentangle. In the Tarot pack, which has been used immemorially by gypsies and others for divination purposes, it survives as an alternative to the Dish, one of the four suits (Miss Jessie Weston, in her *From Ritual to Romance*, suggests that it is a fertility symbol), and also figures in Freemasonry on account of its association with Solomon. Its special functions appear to have been as a guardian of the health and protector against demons.

According to Jewish legends about Solomon, there is no justification for assigning the Pentangle to his seal: the Jewish Encyclopaedia says that it is only in Arabic continuations of the legends that the early, primitive Pentangle occurs, and that it is these versions of the legends that reached the West. But Sir E. A. Wallis-Budge, in his *Amulets and Superstitions*, suggests that the hexagram, or, in Jewish parlance, the Star of David, is a later modification of the Pentangle or Pentacle. However, the Pentacle, containing the ineffable name of God – YHWH (Yahweh or Jehovah) – does appear in the Kabbalah, and representations of it occasionally figure in synagogues. A friend of mine interested in such things writes: 'I've a feeling that in his *degenerate* days Solomon used the device of the 5-pointed star as a defence against demons – neglecting thus the *spiritual* device of his father's "Star of David".' This accords well with the foregoing.

More immediately relevant to our inquiry is the fact that the Pentangle seems to have been known as 'The Druid's Foot'; and also the fact that English folk dancers, at the end of one of their sword-dances, interlock their wooden swords in the form of a pentangle, hold it aloft and cry, 'A Nut! A Nut' (Knot). This is interesting evidence of the existence, in the West, of the pentangle before Christian tradition connected it with Solomon as an important element in his triumph over evil, and later adapted it as a symbol for various precious Christian memories, as it is used in our poem. Professor Tolkien remarks that the Pentangle was a mystic symbol, widely known in the Middle Ages, which comprehended most of the virtues and had power to ward off spirits. Yet Sir Israel

Gollancz, in his notes on *Sir Gawain*, writes: 'According to the O.E.D. this is the only medieval example of the word, or any other compound of pente-, except Pentecost, Pentapolis. The next example of "pentangle" is 1646.' The sign must have had another name: as the Druid's Foot it is mentioned by Goethe and described by Grimm, but I can find no English reference.

MORGAN THE FAY

THE title 'goddess', which is first found applied to Morgan in Giraldus Cambrensis, the twelfth-century Welsh writer, shows her to be related to the Irish goddess of battle, Morrigu, who opposed Cuchulain with her enchantments just as Morgan opposes Arthur and his court. Her warlike attributes are preserved in the story of Sir Peredur, who was trained in arms by nine sorceresses. She has been traced farther back still, to the Celtic goddess Matrona, who was worshipped from northern Italy to the mouth of the Rhine and gave her name to the Marne. Her connexion with water is found everywhere. The mermaids of the Breton coast, who entice fishermen, either killing them with their watery embraces or dragging them down to eternal bliss in their submarine palaces, are 'Morgans'.

Morgan is also related to the Welsh lake fairies who, having ensnared their human lovers, lay prohibitions upon them, and desert them when the prohibitions are broken. One of these fairies, called Modron, has healing powers, which may account for the role of Morgan in Arthurian legend. Morgan lives in an island paradise with eight sisters, and treats Arthur's wounds. As one of the three queens who, in Malory, carry away the dying Arthur in their ship, she retains this exploit, although later tradition presents her as totally hostile to Arthur.

Her enmity to the Round Table is variously accounted for. One legend makes her reveal Lancelot's adultery with Guinevere by giving King Arthur a magical drink which opened his eyes to the perfidy of his wife and friend, while another causes her to be banished from court for having an intrigue with the knight Guiomar. That Guinevere was instrumental in exposing the affair explains

Morgan's special hatred for the queen, which is mentioned in many works besides *Sir Gawain and the Green Knight*. After being banished, Morgan built a valley chapel from which none who had been untrue in love, having entered, could escape. The Green Chapel may owe its origin to this story, for it was specifically to test the chastity of Arthur's knights, which she delighted in attacking, that Morgan built her chapel.

Morgan, being a powerful enchantress, could naturally change her shape. A sinister aspect of her, which presumably underlies the many references to her appearing, as in *Sir Gawain*, as an ugly old woman, is the Welsh Gwrach y Rhibyn, a hideous hag dressed in black, who might be seen by water, splashing herself, or dipping and raising herself in a pool. But Morgan's extreme ugliness and great age are seen by the Christian romancers Platonically, as a direct result of her dealings with the devil. She came by her '*chair ridée*' and '*mamelles pendantes*' through lechery and black magic.

MERLIN

THERE is a huge medieval literature on the subject of Merlin. Possibly his origin is as a royal bard of noble blood in sixth-century Wales. He is supposed to have been present at the battle of Ardderyd (574) between the northern Welsh and the Celts of Scotland, and is said to have gone mad at the sight of the slaughter. He became a solitary 'wild man of the woods', living on roots and berries, and began his career of prophecy and second sight. He prophesied three deaths for a boy, and was justified when the child fell from a rock, was hanged from a tree by his feet, and was drowned because his head was under water. He laughed three times, once at a supposedly virtuous queen whom he knew to have a lover, once at a beggar whom he knew to be sitting over buried treasure, and once at a youth who was carrying some new shoes and who, Merlin knew, would not live to wear them. A similar story is told about Solomon: it may derive ultimately from India. In the same story Merlin dallies with a maid under a tree, an episode which was possibly the source of the Arthurian story of his becoming infatuated with Nimue, an aspect of Morgan the Fay. She enchants him under a whitethorn in the forest of Broceliande, extracts a charm from him and uses it to shut him up in a rock.

Geoffrey of Monmouth incorporated this very old Welsh material in his *Vita Merlini*, in which Merlin is a bard and a prophet, and in his *Historia*, where Merlin is associated with Arthur's court and made a wizard. Merlin is credited with having brought the Giants' Dance (Stonehenge) from Ireland to its present site, with having been instrumental in causing Uther to beget Arthur and institute the Round Table, and with arranging the sword-in-the-stone test for

Arthur's succession. Merlin's supernatural powers are explained partly by his having no mortal for a father, his parents having been a nun and a devil. Robert de Borron, the French poet, who based his 'Merlin' largely on a version of Geoffrey of Monmouth's work, grafted on to the wizard a traditional legend of the begetting of the Antichrist. Accordingly, in some works, Merlin is a Power of Darkness. He has been linked with a Breton wizard, and conjectured as the cultural descendant of a British god who was worshipped at Stonehenge. He even becomes a figure in Scots folk-lore; in the ballad *Child Rowland*, he is a warlock who rescues King Arthur's daughter from Fairyland. He survived as a figure in popular legend, and is mentioned twice by Shakespeare.

But it is Malory's Merlin, with his wonder-working on behalf of Arthur, and his tragic defeat at the hands of the seductive Nimue, who dominates our imagination. His fall seems to typify the collapse of the ancient magic and the glories and mysteries it had made possible.

EXTRACTS FROM THE ORIGINAL POEM

PART ONE, STANZA IX: *The green hair of the knight and his horse*

Wel gay watȝ þis gome   gered in grene
& þe here of his hed   of his hors swete;
Fayre fannand fax   vmbefoldes his schulderes;
A much berd as a busk   ouer his brest henges,
Þat wyth his hiȝlich here,   þat of his hed reches,
Watȝ euesed al vmbetorne,   abof his elbowes,
Þat half his armes þer-vnder   were halched in þe wyse
Of a kyngeȝ capados,   þat closes his swyre.
Þe mane of þat mayn hors   much to hit lyke,
Wel cresped & cemmed   wyth knottes ful mony,
Folden in wyth fildore   aboute þe fayre grene,
Ay a herle of þe here,   an oþer of golde;
Þe tayl & his toppyng   twynnen of a sute,
& bounden boþe wyth a bande   of a bryȝt grene,
Dubbed wyth ful dere stoneȝ,   as þe dok lasted;
Syþen þrawen wyth a þwong,   a þwarle-knot alofte,
Þer mony belleȝ ful bryȝt   of brende golde rungen.
Such a fole upon folde,   ne freke þat hym rydes,
Watȝ neuer sene in þat sale   wyth syȝt er þat tyme,
       With yȝe.
   He loked as layt so lyȝt,
   So sayd al þat hym syȝe;
   Hit semed as no mon myȝt
   Vnder his dyntteȝ dryȝe.

PART TWO, STANZA X: *Sir Gawain's northward journey*

Mony klyf he ouerclambe   in contrayeȝ straunge,
Fer floten fro his frendeȝ   fremedly he rydeȝ.
At vche warþe oþer water   þer þe wyȝe passed,
He fonde a foo hym byfore,   bot ferly hit were,
& þat so foule & so felle   þat feȝt hym byhode.
So mony meruayl bi mount   þer þe mon fyndeȝ,
Hit were to tore for to telle   of þe tenþe dole.
Sumwhyle wyth wormeȝ he werreȝ,   & with wolues als,
Sumwhyle wyth wodwos   þat woned in þe knarreȝ,
Boþe wyth bulleȝ & bereȝ   & boreȝ oþerquyle,
& etayneȝ þat hym anelede,   of þe heȝe felle;
Nade he ben duȝty & dryȝe,   & dryȝtyn had serued,
Douteles he hade ben ded   & dreped ful ofte.
For werre wrathed hym not so much,   þat wynter **was wors,**
When þe colde cler water   fro þe cloudeȝ schadde,
& fres er hit falle myȝt   to þe fale erþe;
Ner slayn wyth þe slete   he sleped in his yrnes
Mo nyȝteȝ þen innoghe   in naked rokkeȝ,
Þer as claterande fro þe crest   þe colde borne renneȝ,
& henged heȝe ouer his hede   in hard ysse-ikkles.
Þus in peryl & payne   & plyteȝ ful harde
Bi contray cayreȝ þis knyȝt   tyl krystmasse euen,
      Al one;
      Þe knyȝt wel þat tyde
      To Mary made his mone,
      Þat ho hym red to ryde
      & wysse hym to sum wone.

PART THREE, STANZA IV: *The Lady's first visit to Sir Gawain*

'God moroun, sir Gawayn,'   sayde þat gay lady,
'ȝe are a sleper vnslyȝe,   þat mon may slyde hider.

Now ar ȝe tan astyt,   bot true vs may schape,
I schal bynde yow in your bedde,   þat be ȝe trayst.'
Al laȝande þe lady   lauced þo bourdeȝ.
'Goud moroun, gay,'   quoþ Gawayn þe blyþe,
'Me schal worþe at your wille,   & þat me wel lykeȝ,
For I ȝelde me ȝederly   & ȝeȝe after grace,
& þat is þe best, be my dome,   for me byhoueȝ nede.'
& þus he bourded aȝayn   with mony a blyþe laȝter.
'Bot wolde ȝe, lady louely,   þen leue me grante,
& deprece your prysoun   & pray hym to ryse,
I wolde boȝe of þis bed   & busk me better,
I schulde keuer þe more comfort   to karp yow wyth.'
'Nay, for soþe, beau sir,'   sayd þat swete,
'ȝe schal not rise of your bedde,   I rych yow better,
I schal happe yow here   þat oþer half als,
& syþen karp wyth my knyȝt   þat I kaȝt haue;
For I wene wel, iwysse,   sir Wowen ȝe are,
þat alle þe worlde worchipeȝ,   quereso ȝe ride;
Your honour, your hendelayk   is hendely praysed
With lordeȝ, wyth ladyeȝ,   with alle þat lyf bere.
& now ȝe ar here, iwysse,   & we bot oure one;
My lorde & his ledeȝ   ar on lenþe faren,
Oþer burneȝ in her bedde,   & my burdeȝ als,
þe dor drawen & dit   with a derf haspe.
& syþen I haue in þis hous   hym þat al lykeȝ,
I schal ware my whyle   wel quyl hit lasteȝ,
            With tale.
        ȝe ar welcum to my cors,
        Yowre awen won to wale,
        Me behoueȝ of fyne force
        Your seruaunt be, & schale.'